"Philip Galanes has made a name for himself as a weekly columnist doling out important advice on social etiquette and now has collected all this wisdom in one terrific book called *Social Q's*. But all this leaves me to wonder what an expert on social etiquette was thinking when he asked a busy woman in the throes of redecorating her apartment to take valuable time away from her rabbit to write a book blurb."

—**Amy Sedaris**

"*Social Q's* by Philip Galanes is the one book you need to help guide you through some of life's toughest social challenges! It's smart, funny, and incredibly practical."

—**Peter Walsh, *New York Times* bestselling author of *Lighten Up* and *It's All Too Much***

"Philip knows his way around an awkward situation—but enough about us!"

—**Kathie Lee & Hoda**

"The *New York Times* advice-meister plumbs problems with verve and attitude in an almost interactive way. *Social Q's* touches all the bases (including new ones, like social media) with a light-hearted, entertaining approach. Philip Galanes could easily be the love child of Emily Post and David Sedaris."

—**Margo Howard, "Dear Margo" advice columnist (formerly "Dear Prudence") for Creators Syndicate and wowowow.com**

"I love Philip Galanes's *New York Times* column! And the book is a must! *Social Q's* is a beacon of light in the foggy haze of today's world."

—**Jessica Seinfeld**

"Zesty, zingy, zippy, zany. Everything I want to say about the funny and very talented Philip Galanes starts with the letter z. He and *Social Q's* are truly zonderful."

**—Henry Alford, humorist and author of**
***How to Live: A Search for Wisdom from Old People***
***(While They Are Still On This Earth)***

"Life in the 21st century is one rude awakening after another. But now we have Philip Galanes's *Social Q's* to the rescue—very smart, very funny advice for sidestepping any etiquette A-bomb."

**—Kendall Farr, author of *The Pocket Stylist* and *Style Evolution***

"*Social Q's* is a hilarious set of solutions to all the problems we're lucky to have. A must-read survival guide."

**—Christian Landers, author of *Stuff White People Like***

"Consider *Social Q's* your funny, wise and indispensable guide for honing, improving and finessing YOU—your own special creation!"

**—George Wayne, contributing editor, *Vanity Fair***

# SOCIAL

# Q's

## HOW *to* SURVIVE
## *the* QUIRKS, QUANDARIES,
## *and* QUAGMIRES
## *of* TODAY

# PHILIP GALANES

Simon & Schuster Paperbacks

New York  London  Toronto  Sydney  New Delhi

For Mary Suh and Laura Marmor,
my staunch editors at the New York Times,
and especially for Social Q's readers, whose prolific
(and terrific) questions have given me a second act.

Simon & Schuster Paperbacks
1230 Avenue of the Americas
New York, NY 10020

First Simon & Schuster trade paperback edition November 2012

SIMON & SCHUSTER PAPERBACKS and colophon are registered
trademarks of Simon & Schuster, Inc.

For information about special discounts for bulk purchases,
please contact Simon & Schuster Special Sales at
1-866-506-1949 or business@simonandschuster.com.

The Simon & Schuster Speakers Bureau can bring authors
to your live event. For more information or to book an event,
contact the Simon & Schuster Speakers Bureau at
1-866-248-3049 or visit our website at www.simonspeakers.com.

Designed by Ruth Lee-Mui

Manufactured in the United States of America

1  3  5  7  9  10  8  6  4  2

The Library of Congress has cataloged the hardcover edition as follows:

Galanes, Philip.
Social Qs : how to survive the quirks, quandaries, and quagmires of today /
Philip Galanes.—1st ed.
p.  cm.
1. Etiquette—Humor.   2. Manners and customs—Humor.   I. Title.
PN6231.E8G35   2011
395.0207—dc22                                        2011015685

ISBN 978-1-4516-0578-5
ISBN 978-1-4516-0579-2 (pbk)
ISBN 978-1-4516-0580-8 (ebook)

Social Q's is a registered trademark of
The New York Times Company and is used with permission.

Illustration credits can be found on page 259.

# Contents

· · · · · · · · · · · · · · · · · · · · · · · · ·

**Part 7: Getting Lovey-Dovey**

**Part 8: Getting Through Our Big Days**

# SOCIAL

. . . . . . . . . . . . . . . . . . . . . . . . . . .

# Not Your Mummy's Advice Column

What should I do?

> I get it all day long.

> I'm pretty sure the woman who swims laps next to me at the Y is peeing in the pool. What should I do?

It started a few years back, when I began the Social Q's advice column for the Sunday Styles section of the *New York Times*.

> My boyfriend has an identical twin that I'm strangely hotter for than I am for him. What should I do?

Since then, the questions come faster than a drunken starlet behind the wheel of a speeding Maserati.

My dad seems to have mixed up my cell phone number with the number of the woman he's seeing behind my mother's back. He sends *her* sexy texts that are freaking *me* out. What should I do?

At the outset, I was afraid that *Times* readers might play it safe, bringing me their old-fashioned etiquette conundrums or mild "Dear Abby" conflicts: When do I use that teeny-tiny fork? What's the right paper stock for my wedding invitation?

Who cares?

And it turns out, I needn't have worried.

My sister goes to work looking like a hooker. What should I do?

From the very beginning, readers set a thoroughly modern tone for my Social Q's column. They write in from all over—people of every age, gender, geography, and social background. And they stride happily to the very edges of our brave new world: where nonstop technology and never-ending pop culture and the once-separate realms of personal and public space have exploded all over each other, pushing us into each other's faces in ways that Grammy and Gramps could never have imagined.

Accidental sexy text messages from our father . . . hello?!

These candid questions demand payback, in spades. So my job is to rush in where angels fear to tread, doling out advice that's tart but tender—and not above the occasional bitch slap. In short, I try to be the best friend you've never met.

The walking wounded must be comforted, of course, and grievous wrongdoers must be spanked. But these are complicated times—and we've all done a thing (or three) we shouldn't have—so I'm not shy about pointing out the good qualities in bald-faced liars. (Maybe they're lying to save our feelings?) And a Goody Two-Shoes reeking of sanctimony has little to look forward to from me but a Krystle Carrington chop across the cheek.

And that's how Social Q's was born, starting with the very first question and answer:

Q My boyfriend assumed I was Jewish when we met on JDate, a website for Jewish singles. I didn't correct him at the time because I was afraid he'd dump me. Now, months later, I'm afraid he's going to dump me because I didn't tell the truth. I really like this guy. What should I do?

—*Christiana, New York City*

A Listen up, Golda (L)eir. In case you hadn't noticed, there's a wee difference between letting an awkward moment pass and masquerading as a Jew for months. Where to next, Gay.com?

I know it can be hard, living as a single in a world full of doubles. But you didn't just fail to "correct" your beau. You lied, having calculated that he might not like the truth. And that's a surefire way to sabotage a relationship.

Clear the air as soon as possible: Just sit your guy down and apologize. Explain that you were feeling vulnerable, but don't let it sound like an excuse—or worse, an attempt to shift the blame to him for making you feel that way. Remember, you'll be one short step from "freak show" when you finally come clean, and you still have to convince him that your lie was an aberration.

He may be furious, or decide you're too manipulative to date, but there's a chance he'll be flattered by the lengths you went to win him over. And who knows? He may have a whopper to get off his chest too.

P.S. What kind of Jew is named "Christiana"?

## *Social Q's:* The Book

Here's the thing: Deep down, we all *want* to do the right thing. But in this age of texting and tweeting, online dating and "Real Housewives of One Too Many Cities," things can get complicated—fast. And when they do, or when you can't even picture what the "right thing" might look like, that's when you've stumbled into Social Q's territory.

Lucky for you, you're not alone anymore.

I've sifted through years of columns (and thousands of questions I haven't had space to answer)—hunting for patterns and culling my sagest advice—to help you navigate the horrible range of awkward moments we all suffer through right now: at home, at work, online, and (even more frequently these days) in the crossroads. From hotsy-totsy bosses on Facebook to scorched-earth exes moving in across the hall.

In this book, chapter by chapter, we'll visit the awkward nooks and crannies of our daily lives, from the moment you wake up (and hopefully, brush your teeth) to your last act of waking consciousness (checking your Match.com mailbox, of course). I'll give you some tools and techniques for making those sticky situations less so. And in the process, I'll answer a raft of illustrative Social Q's from my intrepid readers at the *New York Times*.

But before we begin, I need to ask a favor . . .

### *Starting Principle: Forget Everything You Know!*

Well, not everything, just that little thing we learned in third grade about treating everyone the same.

Because that's crazy talk!

Our country may be founded on the proposition that "all men are created equal," but that hardly means we're all the same. Simply put: Handling a stinky boss is just plain different from handling a smelly housekeeper. (I'm sorry, but it is.) And the faster you master the difference, the sweeter-smelling the world will be.

Navigating the Black Forest of awkward moments demands a gimlet-eyed assessment of who we are versus who the other guy is. Angelina Jolie is not the girl next door, and Reese Witherspoon never plays the sexy stripper. Self-knowledge allows them to choose their roles wisely—and figure out how much of their clothing to keep on.

The same goes for the rest of us. If you're the smartest-gal-in-the-room type, the best response to your awkward problem won't be the same as for the people pleaser down the hall. Our personalities establish the parameters of our most plausible behavior. Because the Bible was right: Leopards do not change their spots—not without laser surgery anyway.

And who is the *other guy*, by the way: a microphone-grabbing Kanye West or a poor little Taylor Swift? (Or for the old folks: a booming Barry White or a high-pitched Joni Mitchell, preciggies.) Is your opponent a teeny-tiny Olsen twin, while we tower over her like LeBron James? Or is she the dragon lady CEO, playing against our milquetoast from the mailroom?

Responding to life's thorniest problems is not a one-size-fits-all proposition. It requires a keen awareness of who we are in relation to other people. Call it contextual IQ. And the more we hone it, the more likely we are to skate over life's thinnest ice without plunging into freezing water and ruining our makeup.

So armed, *Social Q's* will guide us toward our best behavior, helping us navigate the trickiest obstacle courses we can stumble into, and increasing the likelihood of making it through the day in one piece.

Sound good?

Okay, let's get started. And please don't forget to turn off your cell phone, pager, and other portable mobile devices.

# PART 1

Getting Ready

# When Good Hygiene Goes Bad

*Dog Breath and B O and Snot, Oh My!*

Q My assistant is a train wreck: long, greasy hair pulled back into a ponytail, not a stitch of makeup, and dumpy clothes with food stains down the front. I try to set a good example, but she doesn't take the hint.

Yesterday was the last straw. She wore open-toed shoes that showed dirty, unkempt feet. I thought I'd be sick! This young woman wants to move into the business world once she finishes her MBA. Shouldn't I speak with her to help her on her way?

—*Alexandra, Chicago*

A Come off it, Boss Lady! You're not nearly as concerned with Miss Greasy-Haired, Scurfy-Toe's career advancement as you are grossed out by her, right? (Thought so.) Better to keep quiet for the moment.

We don't get to weigh in with people just because they disgust us. There has to be some health risk to them or others, or a close, personal relationship to call on. (Or at least, a certainty that we can run faster than they can!)

But never fear, there's another way to skin this filthy cat: If your assistant considers you a mentor—if she asks for career advice or solicits your opinion—jump right in. Try: "You know, Susie, bad presentation can be a big hindrance to women in the workplace. You may want to keep that in mind."

Just make sure, before opening your mouth, that it's your assistant's interests that are spurring you on, and not your gag reflex.

The world is filled with gorgeousness: blooming roses and verdant meadows, pretty people riding horseback.

But for every pale-pink peony in the world, Social Q's readers have isolated approximately three thousand instances of repulsive behavior: gassy bosses, lice-ridden schoolkids, and restaurant workers who skip out of the bathroom without so much as a backward glance at the sink, much less giving their hands a thorough scrub.

We've had enough!

In the (almost) words of Rodgers and Hammerstein:

> *Fingers up noses, and dog breath on sisters,*
> *Boyfriends with B O, and pasta in whiskers;*
> *Kiddies who sneeze on us from here to Beijing,*
> *These are a few of our least favorite things!*

But when, exactly, can we speak up about bad hygiene, and with whom? Does it take more than a copy of our birth certificate and an offense to one of our five senses? Unfortunately, it does.

Well, how much more? That, my friend, is the question at hand.

Happily, I've developed an easy, three-part test to help us know when we're entitled to set filthy people straight.

### No. 1: Is Anyone's Health at Risk? (And I Don't Mean, Are You About to Vomit Because You're So Grossed Out?)

Is the bad hygiene in question threatening anyone's health, or are you merely disgusted by it? If a person could get sick, give yourself one point. If not, score it a zero. (Don't worry, this test doesn't require a score of 100 percent to speak up. There may be other reasons to weigh in—since I know you're dying to.)

For instance:

My very nice boss often comes out to my cubicle to chat. He proceeds to cough and sneeze on me and my things without covering his mouth or using a handkerchief. I'm starting to feel like I work in a petri dish. Can I speak up?

Please pass the Purell!

See a health risk here? I can. I feel like I'm coming down with something, and I haven't even met this boss. So give yourself 1 point out of a possible perfect score of 3.

Here's another:

My best friend's cat has the run of her house. She lets it walk all over her kitchen counters and stove. It even jumps onto the table during meals. My friend thinks this is cute; I'm appalled. Cats are in and out of their litter boxes all day long and lick themselves to distraction. Don't I have a right to meals that are prepared and eaten in a more hygienic environment?

Survey says, Holy Hair Ball!

No question, cats on the dinner table are disgusting, but there's probably not much chance of becoming sick from your furry dinner companion—even though a single strand of cat hair in my Caesar salad would push me right over the edge. So let's score this one a (grudging) zero: no health risk.

And one more for good measure:

My brand-new boyfriend, who looks a little like Jared Leto, constantly borrows my laptop. He snacks on sticky foods, then licks his fingers—which he puts all over my keyboard. Isn't this unhealthy?

Probably for the keyboard. But as long as you're making out with this guy and trading saliva with him directly, there's probably no increased health risk from indirect contact with his dried-up saliva on your computer. It's gross, for sure, but score it a zero for health risk. (Sorry. But hearty congratulations on snagging a hottie!)

So, with health risk locked in, let's move on to the second question.

### No. 2: Who's in Charge Around Here?

You know those bumper stickers: "Some days you're the fire hydrant; some days you're the dog," "Some days you're the windshield; some days you're the bug," "Some days you're the statue; some days you're the pigeon"?

You get the point.

We enjoy different levels of power in our different relationships, and sometimes, power shifts within a relationship. Bob the Boss may hold the cards at the office, but not after you take another job across town. Jimmy the Summer Intern works for you, and since he also wants to sleep with you, you pretty much own his ass. Your sister, Sarah, and you stand on relatively equal footing, but the simplest suggestion to your brother, Jack, sends him into a tailspin (especially since his divorce).

With power comes the prerogative to speak, often without suffering terrible consequences. (Not that you should!) And with weakness comes a greater need to ingratiate and please. Figuring out where the power lies in that hygiene debacle will help us decide whether to weigh in.

So who's got the power: you or your filthy cohort?

Let's review the preceding scenarios with an eye to identifying the clout. Give yourself another point if you have as much, or more, power than the other guy, and no points if he or she has more power than you.

Sad to say, Sneezy the Boss, who coughs all over us and our desk, has the upper hand here, right? Unless we've got some serious dirt on him, he could probably send us packing on a whim. No additional point.

We're probably on more equal footing with our "best friend," Carla the Cat Lover, whose pesky feline has just started licking the crumbs from the top of the toaster. Let's give ourselves a point.

And the same goes for our hot new boyfriend, the Jared Leto look-alike. Notwithstanding the urban legends about gals getting struck by lightning easier than finding a mate, Laptop Linda seems to be doing just fine. She should tread carefully, since it's a "brand-new" relationship, but I'd still give her (and her sticky laptop) a point.

So, with the health risk and power dynamic of this hygiene fiasco locked down, on to the final question:

### No. 3: Risk Assessment 101—Will There Be "Backdraft"?

The third and final question is the most delicate: What are the risks of speaking up? Will the other person welcome our suggestion for more sanitary living? Or hear our statement as unwarranted criticism or attack?

We're all familiar with the well-known genre of firefighter films, and the moment at which our brave hero—played by Kurt Russell or Denis Leary or any action star of the moment—innocently opens a door inside a burning house and is thrown halfway across the room, explosive flames licking his taut tushie.

It's called backdraft, and we need to guard against it in these hygiene scenarios every bit as much as Mark Wahlberg does. The last thing we want is our smelly cohort thundering back at us with rage.

Assessing the level of risk is a function of how much goodwill we have stored up with this other person, and even more importantly, how attached he or she is to the filthy habit in question.

Give yourself one last point if you believe you can make your plea for cleaner living without becoming subject to fierce counterattack—or a bloody nose.

Drumroll, please, for the big finish: If your total score is 2 out of 3 (or better), feel free to air your concern to the dirty bird, trying to be as tactful as possible. But if your score is less than 2 out of 3, file your would-be suggestion under Gross Things I Guess I'll Keep to Myself.

With Sneezy the Boss, for instance, we may be the *only* person who can make this point: *Stop coughing on us, as if we were merely an extension of you, like some sort of vestigial limb. We're your assistant, dude, not your spittoon!* (But sweeter, of course!)

Sneezy is the boss, though, after all, so we run the risk of alienating him and having to file for unemployment insurance. But the assistant says he's a nice boss. So, given our legitimate health concern and the reasonableness of the request, I'd assess the risk as relatively low and award us another point, bringing the tally to 2 out of 3.

So let it rip! Try smiling: "Quite a cold you have there, Boss Man! Would you like a box of Kleenex for your office?" That should do the trick. And as an added incentive, underscore the value—to him—of your good health: "I want to stay fit as a fiddle to keep your expense reports up to date!"

Kitty Cat Lover poses a different problem: She's our best friend, so we probably have loads of goodwill with her, and our request to keep Puss in Boots off the table during mealtime could not be more reasonable. But in my experience, people's pets are like bona fide members of their family. And asking her to quarantine her cat is like asking your sister to put her toddler in storage. (You remember how that went!)

So, unfair as it may seem, I fear a massive counterinsurgency by asking her to keep the cat at bay: big risk. No more points, I'm afraid, bringing the grand total to a mere 1 out of 3.

I'd keep your lips zipped—and avoid mealtime at the Kitty Castle. Invite your best friend out to dinner instead. Just think of the incremental cost of restaurants as being offset by lower dry-cleaning bills, now that you won't be covered head to toe in cat hair every time you see her.

Finally, we come to Jared Leto, chomping on chicken wings that are finger-lickin' good, then surfing the web on our laptop. Not much to fear, right? He's our boyfriend. What's more, he's probably never stopped to think about how gross his habit is, and won't mind too much when we point it out. Give us another point, for 2 out of 3.

Swing for the fences, girlfriend: "Sweetie, when you lick your fingers and type like that, you're sort of marinating my keyboard in spit. Do you think you could knock it off?"

Now that you've got a few under your belt, consider one last hygiene horror:

Q I have a cousin who I'm very close with. His breath reeks—not so bad that you notice it from across the room, but bad enough to curl your hair when you're standing next to him. I think it's the reason he's never found a long-term girlfriend. None of his dates seem to go anywhere. Should I talk to him about his breath?

Before you answer, make sure to run through our three-part hygiene test:

1. Health risk? ❏
2. Power in the relationship? ❏
3. Possible backdraft? ❏

Once you've worked out your answer, turn the page to look at mine. (No cheating!)

Hello, nuclear-strength Altoids!

In most cases, I'd suggest holding your tongue—and your nose. But you've distinguished yourself from the garden-variety hygiene hawk. You're worried about your cousin's long-term happiness, not fainting from the miserable stench.

Go ahead, make his day. Say, "Cuz, I've noticed your breath has taken a turn for the stinky. Maybe you should check in with your dentist about this."

It may be as simple as brushing more often, but that grosses me out. I prefer to think he has a medical condition that will be rectified with pills and shiny silver implements.

So, how'd you do?
Check the box that fits:

❏ Great!   ❏ I'm not sure I agree   ❏ Is it too late for a refund?

It may not work every time, but at least we've got a simple rubric for handling those icky hygiene disasters that we run across every day.

Feeling any cleaner?

Me too.

Shall we try one more for good measure?

Q I work the second shift in an office where cubicles are shared. The fellow who uses my cubicle in the first shift has a luxurious beard. Every night, I come to work and find beard hairs all over my desk and keyboard. I find this incredibly disgusting. Is there a polite way of asking him to clean up after himself?

—Marci

A How about weaving those molted whiskers into a wreath that you can hang from your shared cubicle wall, with a bit of verse attached:

> Your beard is handsome,
> And deserves an award.
> But on your face,
> Not in my keyboard.
> Don't forget to tidy!

And if you're short on time, feel free to skip the wreath.

# 2

. . . . . . . . .

# Beauty Experiments

*Or, Who Died and Made You Estée Lauder?*

**Q** A woman I know a little, but like a lot, had a boob job. It's *really* noticeable, but she's never mentioned the procedure or asked for my opinion. Should I compliment her on her new look anyway, even though I'm not so sure it was a good idea? It feels awkward to say nothing, but even more awkward to bring it up. What should I do?

—*Jackie, Ohio*

**A** There are two kinds of people in the world, Jackie O(hio). The better kind are the ones who bump into a new set of knockers on the street—or a criminal haircut or even a volcanic zit at the end of a nose—and act as if nothing were amiss.

These are the same folks, by the way, who walk past Britney Spears at Kentucky Fried Chicken without giving her a second glance. I've never actually met such a person.

The rest of us telegraph what we see: by gazing at the new rack for a millisecond too long, or looking too studiously away. Don't even bother. Your pal will sense what's going on and awkwardness will ensue.

Don't mention the new boobs either. That might make her feel self-conscious—though she's the one who opted for Double Ds, right? Go with a general-purpose compliment: "Wow, you're looking well today."

Trust me, your pal will know exactly what you mean. And you'll have left the choice to her. She can engage you in a pointed conversation about the ta-tas, or simply appreciate the compliment (and your tact).

And under no circumstances should you criticize an *acquaintance's* new look. Who cares what you think? (Nor should you utter the name Pamela Anderson.)

The flip side of good hygiene—that regimen of chores we follow to keep ourselves clean and fragrant, as well as give a semblance of good health—is the "Beauty Experiment": that purely optional tweak or change we make in our appearance to enhance our allure.

We all do them: from concealing blemishes with flesh-colored goop, to coaxing out the tawny lowlights in our hair. (And that's just the men!)

There's nothing wrong with beauty tweaks. Far from it! Whether it's under the guise of Oprah's "Live Your Best Life" or the U.S. Army's "Be All You Can Be," we Americans are suckers for self-improvement. And what could be more improving than a physical upgrade? It may be what's on the inside that counts, but it's the outside that shows.

There's one teeny problem, though: Like any experiment, whether conducted in a chemistry lab or in front of your bathroom vanity, some beauty experiments fail. Others never should have been undertaken in the first place. And some are so egregious that they constitute crimes under state and federal laws. (Just what *is* that you're injecting into your frown lines, Mrs. Robinson?)

Furthermore, ill-conceived or badly executed beauty experiments can subject us to embarrassment and even ridicule. (Don't make me show you pictures of that spray-on tan debacle.) So what's a person to do? How do we know whether to proceed with that dye job or nose job or any other job we have in mind—or leave it on the shelf?

If we move forward, and the results are disastrous, what then?

And finally, how should we conduct ourselves when we encounter beauty experiments gone (hideously) wrong out on the street: Should we weigh in or keep our mouths shut?

### Welcome to the Beauty Matrix!

Careful study of the annals of higher mathematics—well, my dog-eared sixth-grade math book—has yielded a formula for deciding whether to pluck or pop, chunk-highlight or grow it out. It's ironic, of course, that the answer to these sensitive questions has been at our disposal from the moment we first needed one. That's right: since the onset of puberty in middle school.

Here's an example:

> I'm a dark-haired girl who's wanted to go blond since the first time I laid eyes on Marcia Brady. All my friends tell me I shouldn't do it, that it's too big a change. But I have a gut feeling I'd look great. I know it's just hair; still, I'd hate to look like a freak for half a year while it grows out. What should I do?
>
> —*CeeCee, Vermont*

In the words of Jan Brady: "Marcia, Marcia, Marcia!"

This is a perfect case for using the Beauty Matrix: CeeCee is ambivalent. Her friends say no, but she's got a lingering desire to go for the gold(en). So what should she do?

I thought you'd never ask!

On a horizontal line (or "x-axis"—ringing any bells?) plot how badly CeeCee wants to take the plunge to Honey Blond.

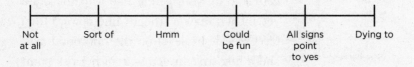

| Not at all | Sort of | Hmm | Could be fun | All signs point to yes | Dying to |

Based on the question, I'd place CeeCee halfway between "Could be fun" and "All signs point to yes." But you don't need to agree with me. Simply mark the point across the range that you think best represents CeeCee's level of desire.

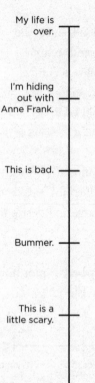

My life is over.

I'm hiding out with Anne Frank.

This is bad.

Bummer.

This is a little scary.

Who cares?

Now, on a vertical line (or y-axis), plot how big a risk this particular beauty experiment is. In other words, how badly will CeeCee take it if the peroxide procedure is a bust? The higher up we go, the bigger the risk.

Based on the language of the question, I'd rank CeeCee's fear factor about midway up the line, at "This is bad." She doesn't seem overly concerned about her friends' warnings or the prospect of failure. And her main worry—the length of time it will take for the blond to grow out—is easily addressed: She can skip back into Frédéric Fekkai and have it dyed dark again.

Now, here comes the big innovation:

Put the horizontal and vertical axes together. (Are you feeling like a math wizard yet?) Then draw a straight line upward from CeeCee's desire level on the horizontal axis, and a line straight across from her risk point on the vertical axis. Eventually the lines will intersect at CeeCee's Decision Point.

Ready for the big finish?

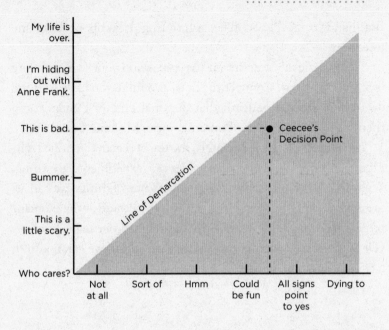

As long as the decision point falls *beneath* the diagonal line that divides the Beauty Matrix in half—the Line of Demarcation—go for it!

And since that's where CeeCee's Decision Point falls, let the bleaching begin! (Just make sure to keep us posted, CeeCee: Do blondes really have more fun—or just a hell of a lot more maintenance?)

But don't take my word for it either. Try the Beauty Matrix yourself: Choose a beauty experiment that you've been contemplating for a while, but can't seem to pull the trigger on. A

Brazilian wax maybe, or an eyelash tinting? How about Restylane injections?

Plot your level of desire on the x-axis and your fear-of-failure level on the y-axis. Connect the dots, and there you have it: If the decision point falls beneath that diagonal Line of Demarcation, then start warming up the Bunsen burners, Madame Curie!

*Important Note:* Unfortunately, the use of pseudoscientific techniques will not eliminate tears when our experiments go wrong. We'll cry like babies! But in the grand scheme of things, we can almost think of those crying jags as worth it, because at the moment of decision, our desire to beautify outweighed our fear of failure. (Or at least it did theoretically, which may be all we can ask from a two-dimensional graph.)

Next stop:

### When Beauty Experiments Go Bad

It was just a matter of time.

When you stop to think of all the aesthetic choices we make in the course of a day (a week, a year), we're lucky not to generate more beauty crises than we do. But when we strike out with a supersized collagen injection to the lips (Hello, Meg Ryan!), or a spotty-leopard spray-on tan (Snooki, my love!), what then?

Easy, breezy, beautiful Cover Girl! Just take a page from John Wayne's book: "Never apologize and never explain."

## Weighing In on the Beauty Fiascos of Others

As critical as we may be of ourselves, Social Q's readers are often even more anxious to criticize others. (Which sounds about right, no?)

A woman I work with plucks her eyebrows way too thin. Wouldn't it be a favor for me to tell her?

Good try! But I'm not sure the word "favor" will spring to mind when you compare her eyebrows to Silly String.

My new boyfriend's pubic bush is wildly overgrown and semi-scary. Can I ask him to trim down there?

Only if you first explain why the grass is always greener (and looks better tended) on the other side of the fence.

My younger sister pierced her lower lip, which is already enough to make me sick, but that little ring is like a magnet for food and saliva. Can I please tell her to take it out?

Chances are, your beauty fiasco isn't as bad as it seems. And even if it is, the rest of us are much too absorbed with our own problems to spend much time worrying about yours. We may not even notice. So why draw our attention to it?

I know it's hard, and that you're dying to bring it up, but trust me: Keep your lips zipped! Better to spend your energy fixing the problem—or in the case of ugly tattoos, trying to rise above them. You have nothing to gain from making your bad haircut the center of attention, and it's only going to make you feel more self-conscious.

You get the point, right?

When you see something ugly, and you're just dying to weigh in, stop! Take a quick jaunt down Memory Lane, first, and revisit the Beauty Matrix, but this time with a twist. On the horizontal axis, plot how horrifying the problem is. And on the vertical axis, plot how well you know the other person.

Like so:

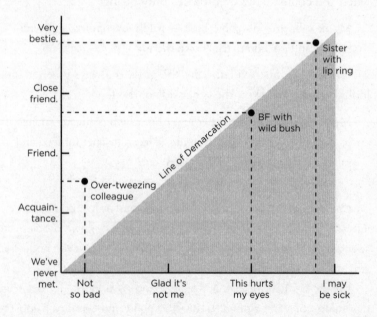

And like before, let the diagonal Line of Demarcation be your guide, as our pseudoscientific nomenclature gives you more confidence than it should. Just cite the Beauty Matrix as you sing out to your boyfriend about his rampant pubes and to your sister with the mangled lip—and damn it to hell for keeping you mum when it comes to your co-worker's skinny eyebrows.

Of course, you might rate these disasters (and characters) differently. That's what makes a horse race. But keep to the grid, unless you just can't help yourself. But in that case, better to invest in a thick skin too, because there's nothing like dishing it out to encourage people to see if we can also take it!

Now that we've analyzed a few Beauty Experiments—both from the perspective of people who've yet to take the plunge, as well as those who've witnessed experiments they don't like the looks of—let's end our discussion with a twist.

Here's a question from a fellow who's already thrown caution to the wind, but isn't sure how to evaluate the fallout. Consider it in light of the issues we've discussed: How much does our fine fellow like the results of his Beauty Experiment? Is he close with the folks who are giving him grief?

After you've come up with your answer, turn the page and take a look at mine:

I'm a well-built man in my fifties. I wear my hair long, past my shoulders, and I love the way it looks and feels. But waiters and other strangers refer to my wife and me as "you girls," which pisses me off. Do I have to cut my hair?

—*Michael, Houston*

Why not try losing the glittery headbands and butterfly barrettes first? They can be awfully distracting.

The problem is that these people aren't really seeing you. The waiters, for instance, are rushing from table to table—thinking of iced tea, and getting to the market in time, and wondering if Bruce Willis really started out this way. They don't mean any offense. They're just self-absorbed like the rest of us. And when they pick up on a female cue—like your lustrous mane—they run with it.

Your odds of changing this dynamic are about as good as Just For Men hair dye being mistaken for a natural color. Don't let it steam you—or prompt you to cut your hair either. The next time someone calls you "little lady," just reply, with a saucy smile, "That's Mr. Little Lady to you."

And remember: You've come out way ahead. Think of all the bald men who'd trade places with you in a hot second.

# If the Shoe Fits, It's Ugly!

*On Fashion Crimes and Misdemeanors*

Q I was running errands in a crowded store and noticed that the woman in front of me was wearing leggings that were much too small for her huge behind. As a result, the leggings were stretched to the point of see-through, and her large white "granny pant-ies" were fully visible. It looked like she was wearing pantyhose! I don't believe this was her intention. And I almost said something to her. Should I have?

—*Rhonda, Dallas*

A Not unless you're the host of one of those horrible "fashion" reality shows and you've run out of young assistants and hopeful designers to beat up on.

You have no relationship with this woman, so you can't possibly know what her intentions were. And apart from an oblique view of the tragic panties, nothing terrible was exposed. (Thank your lucky stars she wasn't wearing a thong!)

So unless you're angling to replace the dearly departed Mr. Blackwell—of the international worst-dressed lists—and prepared to deal with fierce (and nasty) competition from the blogosphere, leave shopping strangers to their own fashion instincts.

You know that expression "You're never fully dressed without a smile"? Well, that may be true, but this chapter is about the ugly dress you're wearing and other fashion catastrophes.

In a practical sense, clothing allows us to express who we are: a suit for the suit; a crown for the crown. Doctors wear lab coats, and firemen wear black rubber boots. It's hard to screw up a uniform, whether formalized into a dress code or consisting of looser principles that are known to all parties. And when we err, people aren't shy about letting us know: *Go home and put on a tie, Wilson.* Or: *You march yourself upstairs, young lady, and make yourself decent! We're going to a restaurant, not a strip club.*

These aren't particularly awkward transactions either. Someone has violated the rules, and someone else is merely pointing it out.

Easy, right? Not so fast . . .

As any schoolgirl who's rolled the waistband of her regulation skirt can tell you, it's possible to follow the rules while still expressing our individual ideas about who we are. That "sixty is the new thirty-five" corporate lawyer in a push-up bra and skirt slit up her thigh, for instance, or the suburban accountant who wears a pork-pie hat and sunglasses—indoors.

These are the fashion faux pas that drive people crazy. (And I have two zillion letters to prove it.)

*She thinks she's so hot!* they write about the sexed-up lawyer. Or, *Go balance your ledgers, hipster wannabe!* of the accountant with Rat Pack dreams.

But let's hit the Pause button for a second. We see all kinds of ugly things—and silly things and unpleasant things—all through the day. For the most part, we simply turn our heads and carry on. What about these fashion flare-ups is so different?

Well, studying the letters, a pattern emerged: It's not about the clothing at all.

The outfits are just a pretext! What really bothers us is the gap between our idea of people and their apparent image of themselves, which we glean from what they're wearing. That woman in the see-through leggings, for instance, thinks her ass is small enough to get away with leggings. We want to take her down a peg.

When we see Plain Janes strutting their stuff like burlesque queens, or white-bread milquetoasts looking too cool for school, we want to tell them, "You're not fooling us for a second! We know who you are, so take off that damn bustier (or dashiki, as the case may be)!"

Fashion may be the inciting factor, but it's not what's really getting under our skin. We like to keep people in tidy boxes: the smart one, the timid one, the one who sings like Michael Bolton.

It confirms our understanding of the world and our place in it. If people color too far outside the lines we've drawn for them, or dress themselves up as different characters, it can feel threatening to us. So we'd rather shove them back into the boxes we've made for them than acknowledge their right to wear whatever ugly, ill-fitting outfit they choose.

Turns out, it's not them; it's us!

And to make matters worse, the Boulevard of Fashion Complaints is a one-way street, and when we're traveling on it, we tend to suffer from selective blindness.

*Why does she wear a bra that's three sizes too small for her, forcing me to watch her fat explode all around it?* asks the guy in the loud Hawaiian shirt and striped pants.

Or *I can't stand the way he unbuttons his shirt down to his navel, so I have to look at his hairy chest all day* says the gal with the furiously coordinated accessories.

Here's the thing: We rarely see our own fashion flubs, though we're quick on the trigger when it comes to those of other people.

What's "fashionable" is what *I'm* wearing. What's "unfashionable" is what *she* has on.

To avoid these pitfalls—of butting in where we don't belong, or acting like we answer to the name Coco Chanel—I've put together a little memory aid to help us navigate the turbulent seas of fashion disasters. Before you say a word about that raspberry beret, just think:

### Tic-Tac-Toe

That's right: Tic-tac-toe, a game so simple only the youngest of children can be bothered to play it. But in our deft hands, a wondrous checklist for all things fashion.

### Tic for Tic(k) a Lock

A small homage to Edith Bunker, Aunt Bee from *Mayberry R.F.D.*, and benevolent librarians the world over, who have used this expression, often with a little "turning the key" hand gesture at the corner of their mouths, to signify the locking of lips.

Keep your mouth shut!

Does it really matter, in the grand scheme of things, that the colors of your sister-in-law's outfit clash? Or that your boss's pants are a tad tight across the seat? Or that your girlfriend's love of floral prints rivals that of Laura Ashley?

Of course it doesn't!

Will it drive you crazy to keep from telling them—or for that matter, the woman sitting at the next table whose blouse is inside out, her Lady Wrangler label for all the world to see? Quite possibly. Does that mean you should speak up, after all? Definitely not! (Especially to the woman in the restaurant, since her dinner companion is probably much better positioned to let her know.) Just leave it alone.

### Tac for Tac(ky) Is Relative

Or, in the huffy words of Imelda Marcos, when pressed about why she owned three thousand pairs of shoes: "I *never* had three thousand pairs of shoes! I only had one thousand and sixty."

Everyone's entitled to their own taste—to decide what looks good on them, and how much is too much.

Did anyone ask for your opinion? (Didn't think so.) And even if they did, be careful. They probably just want a little validation that they're smokin' hot. So give it to them: "I've never seen anything quite like it!"

### Toe for Toe(s) Are One Thing:
### Full Frontal Is Another (and So's Your Mother).

There are two exceptions to the foregoing rules, where butting in is obviously required.

The first is in the case of inadvertent exposure. That clueless old guy who lives next door is walking around the neighborhood in short shorts, with nothing on underneath, and you see a little more of him than you bargained for. What then? Either move or feel free to ask him to invest in a pair of skivvies.

The second exception covers certain inextricably linked, Gordian-knotted twosomes: mothers and daughters (*My fifty-five-year-old mother wants to wear a micromini to meet my boyfriend's parents*), romantic partners (*My husband keeps asking me if his jeans make his ass look big—and they do*), and absolute besties (*My best friend, who is whiter than Vanna White, wears saris more often than Indira Gandhi*).

Try as we might, it's simply not possible to keep our mouths shut with these folks, so don't give yourself a stroke trying. Let loose with the cutting remark—then pay the inevitable price.

We're only human, right?

### Dressed for Success

#### *But Not in Those Flip-Flops, You Aren't!*

It's called "work" for a reason. And the reason is: It's not the beach or the mall or a nightclub or the gym. So why would you go to the office dressed in flip-flops or sweatpants, strapless tops or anything made of Lycra?

These other places are a lot more fun than work, but it's not as if wearing a bikini top is going to transform your cubicle into a beach chair, is it? And your "I'm next on the treadmill" look isn't going to do much to increase the respect that your boss and co-workers have for you either.

Here's what you do: Dress for work like you're going to a fun church: Not too much skin, no micro-minis or leggings, and absolutely no flip-flops.

If this seems too severe, or if it's been a really long time since you've sat in a pew, pick out someone at your office who's doing really well and whom you admire: your boss's boss, maybe, or the head of HR. Then watch how they dress and take your cues from them.

Clothes may not make the man—but they have gotten him a few nice promotions. And I promise you, the people who succeed at work are never the ones who look like they just finished a shift at Scores.

So there you have it. Fashion faux pas handled as easily as tic-tac-toe! Let's try one last question together, and see how you do:

Q I have a gorgeous red dress that I'd like to wear to my best friend's wedding. But my mother told me that it's frowned upon for women to wear red to weddings. I've never heard this rule. Can I disregard it? I don't want to offend.

Remember to keep in mind these principals as you consider your answer:

**Tic** for Tic(k) a Lock.
**Tac** for Tack(y) is Relative; and
**Toe** for Toe(s) are One Thing; Full Frontal is Another (and So's Your Mother).

When you've got your answer, turn the page to compare it with mine.

As long as it's not a wedding-slash-bullfight, you should be fine.

It's sweet of you to worry about giving offense, but don't let old-fashioned rules tie you in knots. Women may have been discouraged from wearing red in olden days because it was considered racy—or worse, associated with prostitutes. But gals couldn't vote in those days, or compete on *American Idol,* either.

So, wear your red dress—unless it makes you look like a hooker, in which case, you'll want to invest in some incredibly high heels as well.

# PART 2

Getting There

# 4

· · · · · · · · ·

# The Court of Public Transportation

*Judge Judy for a Day!*

**Q** I have a mad crush on a fellow commuter that's been brewing for six months now. I see him three or four times a week. Would it be okay for me to approach him on the subway and ask for his number to arrange a date?

—*Brooke, Boston*

**A** It's a free country, Brooke. So as long as you keep your clothes on—and have another way of getting to the office, in case you're thin-skinned—you can proposition anyone you like.

But don't misunderstand me: Even though half the fun of riding public transport is projecting romantic fantasies onto fellow commuters—well, the attractive ones anyway—across-a-crowded-subway plotlines are rarely as successful in real life as they are on the Lifetime Network.

Sometimes a guy just wants to read the paper in the morning, you know? Especially when he's trapped in a car underground, without any means of escape. So, baby steps: Maybe start by smiling at your future husband when you see him on the platform, or asking nonchalantly, "Is it hot down here—or is it just you?"

## All aboard!

What better way to travel—for our pocketbooks and the environment—than by public transportation: via bus, train, or commercial airline (in case the private jet is in the shop for repairs).

Sounds great, right? And it is too—up to the moment when you snag that last seat on the bus, only to discover that the guy sitting next to you is blaring his iPod so loudly that Jay-Z seeps out of his earphones and overtakes your central nervous system. Or until you notice that posse of teenage boys and girls, sitting on the uptown local, while the visibly (and very) pregnant woman standing next to you can't find a seat. Or until the tipsy woman next to you on your flight to China launches into the unabridged story of her marital woes—and is oblivious to every "shut up!" vibe you send her way. Or until the . . .

You get the point.

When it comes to public transportation, it's tricky to know where our rights begin and the rights of fellow travelers leave off. Remember, we're dealing with strangers, for the most part—lots of them!—so we tend to be a little rougher around the edges than we would be with co-workers or neighbors, or someone we're likely to see again soon.

What's more, we're often sharing tight (and uncomfortable) quarters, from which there's no ready means of escape. Does anything crank up the fury meter faster than being packed onto an overheated, slow-moving conveyance with a guy who keeps jamming his elbow into our kidneys? It's inevitable that tempers will flare. So, how do we navigate the turbulence when it does?

## Balancing Our Rights Against Theirs

Take that guy on the subway with the blaring iPod. Please! You remember, the one whose music is seeping out of his headset and onto us, giving us all a headache? Whether or not we ask him to turn down the volume, we can probably all agree that we have the right to speak up.

We live in a country that values freedom of speech. The First Amendment to our Constitution—our very first law—guarantees that no one may restrict our ability to speak up or express ourselves. And if the Supreme Court concluded that the First Amendment allows Nazis to parade through a community filled with Jews and Holocaust survivors (which it did in 1977), then surely it must protect our right to ask our fellow commuters, "Would you turn the *&%$#@* volume down?!"

But the First Amendment also protects the freedom of a guy to listen to a little gangsta rap on his iPod on his way to the office.

So is it a standoff? Of course not.

Our freedom to say and do as we like is not absolute. There are plenty of exceptions. We can't yell "Fire!" in a crowded theater, for instance, without being carted off to jail for reckless endangerment. And we're not allowed to be profane or pornographic either, though most of the reality shows on Bravo do a damn fine job of it. But the exception that best fits the world of public transportation—and applies most neatly to the set of troubles we encounter on planes, trains, and buses—is one that was first described in the 1920s by a Supreme Court justice who was so smart that they named a college after him, Justice Louis Brandeis.

In a flash of common sense, Brandeis laid out the most fundamental right of all: "the right to be let alone"—our freedom to pursue life, liberty, and happiness without unnecessary intrusion by the government or other people. In short, we have the right to go about our business—and ride the train—in relative peace. And by extension, the right to listen to music in peace too.

So how do we square these rights—and behave well? How do we decide whether our right to a peaceful ride outweighs that of our music-loving fellow commuters, and vice versa?

### The Scales of Justice

Well, it's all a balancing act, involving the Scales of Justice. (You know, from the logo on *Law & Order*.) Mr. iPod may have a right to listen to music through earphones, but that's not what he's doing, is it? When his music escapes from those tiny white earbuds, he's forcing everyone to listen to his music, and trampling on our right to be left alone.

The scales of justice are out of whack:

What's more, with a small compromise, we can restore balance (and equity) to the equation, and make sure that everyone's rights are respected. Just tap the rocker gently on his shoulder—because there's no way in Motown he'll ever hear a polite "excuse me" over that throbbing bass line—and say, smiling, "We can all hear your music. Can you turn down the volume, please?"

That's it! No witticism required.

In fact, a smart remark would probably just annoy the guy who wants to rock his playlist all the way to Times Square. As easy as that, the scales of justice are back in balance and (relative) peace is restored to the Uptown Local.

*Important Note*: Please don't confuse the foregoing discussion of justice and our great nation of laws with stupidity. If the guy with the iPod refuses to turn down his music, or becomes menacing, cave immediately! There may be loads of people on that subway car, but very few of them are likely to come to your defense. And let's be honest, even though violent crime underground is rare, it's still a little scary down there, right?

Now let's apply the Scales of Justice to a few more problems that crop up on public transportation. It's a little exercise I call:

### Judge Judy for a Day!

Hitch up your black robe, and get ready to play! Let's see if we can balance the right of one person to do (or say) something against the right of someone else to be left alone.

Let's start with an easy one:

I was standing on a crowded airport shuttle when an elderly, hunched-over couple got on. No one offered them their seats, though they were the oldest and frailest passengers by far. I wasn't sure if the seated people had seen them. I didn't say anything. Should I have?

—*Benjamin, Baltimore*

Does Benjamin have the right to speak up—drawing the elderly couple with osteoporosis to the attention of the younger, lither passengers on the airport shuttle? Of course he does, especially if he's correct in thinking that the other passengers may not have seen the hunched-over couple. He might merely tap a couple of the Jonas Brothers on their shoulders, or ask the elderly folks (in a clear, loud-ish voice so that other passengers can hear him), "Would you like to sit down?"

But doesn't that interfere with the right of younger passengers to be left alone? Technically, sure. Who wants strangers approaching them, asking for favors? And those airline shuttles are first-come, first-served, after all. It's not the youngsters' fault that older (or frailer) passengers get there last.

Still, it's not a big imposition to stand for a few minutes so that less able people can sit. And whether the young 'uns ultimately agree to give up their seats, the request will only take a few seconds. We'll be back to grousing about security delays and lost luggage in no time.

In my view, Benjamin's decision not to speak left the Scales of

Justice out of whack, giving more weight to his fear of bothering other passengers than to his right to speak up on behalf of the weak:

**SPEAK UP**

**LEAVE THE
KIDS ALONE**

### Mind Your Own Beeswax!

There are so many situations in this world where we can be helpful—at the local soup kitchen, or with emergency relief efforts. But there are also times when we should just stay the hell out of it!

A while back, I received a letter from a reader who was extremely annoyed that people in wheelchairs are pushed to the front of the line at customs and immigration in airports. These people, he wrote, "are usually just old or fat, and they look very comfy in their wheelchairs." Why should they be moved ahead of him, he wanted to know—not to mention their healthy family members too?

My advice to Dr. Welby, after thanking him for his crack medical diagnosis, was, Take a Valium and call me in the morning. Still, the newspaper received approximately four billion letters from outraged

But with just a brief interruption of the other passengers, he can restore balance to the Scales of Justice. And those oldsters will be sitting in no time flat!

Let it rip, Benjamin!

There's a caveat, though: What makes us so sure that these older folks need our help to solve their seating problems—or even want to sit, for that matter? (Well, I'm a massive buttinsky. What's your excuse?) They may prefer to stand, or might have asked someone on their own, without any assistance from us.

So be careful. It is close quarters on public transport, and sometimes that can give us the mistaken impression that we're involved

individuals, advocacy groups, and even from a major airline. The letter writers wanted blood!

But here's the thing: Traveling can make us crazy! Too much time on cramped airplanes or in airports without fresh air; waiting on lines that don't seem to make any sense; the near-constant requests to remove, then retie our shoes. All these things can be really, really annoying. So we're inclined to take it out on people—and policies—that are none of our business.

Try not to get too worked up about things you see on public transportation. And when, inevitably, you do, ask yourself, Would this upset me if it weren't two hundred degrees in here, or we weren't twenty-three hours late? Is this any of my business at all?

When it comes to public transportation, take a chill pill. Really.

in questions that are none of our affair. It's good to be part of the solution, of course, but don't jump in too quickly. That "pregnant woman" may just be fat, and the "older man" might not like to think of himself that way.

Be respectful of other people's decisions too. If someone tells you she prefers to stand, leave it alone. Same with younger passengers, who may not jump to their feet just because you ask them to. They may have reasons for sitting that we don't know about. So tread lightly, okay?

On to another example:

I'm a tall girl with long legs. When I sit on airplanes, my knees almost touch the seat in front of me. The last time I flew, the guy reclined his seat, so it was literally pressing into my knees, and his head was practically in my lap! I asked him politely to keep his seat upright, but he refused. What could I have done?

—*Celia, New York City*

Whenever I need a bit more elbow room on a plane, Celia, I find that a loud-ish reference to the airsickness bag usually does the trick!

Celia has the right to ask the fellow in front of her to return his seat toward an upright position: He'd reclined himself right onto her knees! But said fellow, in an audacious display of "the right to be let alone," refused.

The Scales of Justice seem terribly out of whack, no?

The recliner's right to fly in peace can't trump Celia's physical comfort entirely, can it? Of course not.

But here's what you *don't* do: Continue to plead with the guy in front of you, or let that conversation escalate into full-scale war. What good is that going to do? She's already asked, and he's already answered.

Better to move on. Just press the flight attendant button ASAP. Perhaps there's a free seat (with a more reasonable passenger in front of it) elsewhere on the plane. Or perhaps the attendant can coax the passenger in front of Celia to move his seat a little more upright. Sometimes the other guy is going to be a meanie. And in the absence of parachute gear, we simply have to deal with it.

Okay, last one:

Q I saw a nanny on the subway with an infant and a small toddler boy. The nanny gave the boy an apple, but kept snatching it back to eat herself, and yelling at the boy for being upset. Her tone was very nasty. I'm sure the parents would be angry if they knew how their son was being treated. What should I have done?

—*Rachael*

This time, try the analysis on your own. And when you've assessed the Scales of Justice—one party's right to express himself versus the other's right to be left alone (as well as the box "Mind Your Own Beeswax")—turn the page and see if you agree with my conclusion:

THE RIGHT
TO SPEAK UP

THE RIGHT
TO BE
LEFT ALONE

Since we're coming to the story in midstream, Rachael, we can't really tell if we're dealing with Maria von Trapp on a bad day or Bloody Mary, queen of England, on a good one. Let's not judge the nanny on the basis of a single Golden Delicious.

Still, I take your point: It's hard to watch people mistreating animals and small children. But it's even harder to see how a stranger's intervention on a subway car will help matters—or to know, for sure, if help is even needed. She didn't strike the kids, after all.

I'd leave this one alone. If you just can't help yourself, try sidling up to Grouchy Poppins and commiserating with her over how tough toddlers can be. That might defuse the situation. And it certainly beats trailing her for the rest of the day, snapping evidentiary photos of her eating the little boy's string cheese, right?

# 5

· · · · · · · · ·

# When Strangers Get a Little Strange

*On Sidewalks, at Starbucks, and Just Waiting in Line*

Q I was second in line waiting for the cashier at Costco, when a woman asked the guy in front of me if she could go ahead, because she had only one item. He agreed, but I pointed out that she should ask everyone who was waiting. She was cutting in front of all of us, after all. The man got very angry and threatened me. When I didn't back down, he said he'd be waiting for me outside. (Fortunately, he wasn't.) But wasn't I right?

—*Robert, Long Island, NY*

A Ah, you remind me of that old Meg Ryan movie "When High-Minded Met Smackdown." Of course you were right, Robert, but was it worth a possible black eye?

The whole point of good manners is to prevent bumps in the road, or to smooth them over if they can't be avoided. Your statement about the line-hopping was fair, and you did nothing wrong in making it. But when you discovered you were dealing with a hair-triggered hellion, you should have withdrawn immediately. (And probably called for the store manager.)

Otherwise, who knows what injury might have befallen you and the innocent bystanders—and even closer to my heart, those thousand-gallon drums of pistachios that make Costco a heaven on earth?

From close encounters with sidewalk hogs, to the slightly more complicated indignities we suffer at the hands of complete strangers—on the sidewalk, in the dairy aisle of the supermarket, or in line at the bank—figuring out how to handle people we *don't* know can sometimes be more daunting than dealing with boorish friends and nasty neighbors.

Weird, right?

We don't even know these folks. So you'd think that dispatching them would be a breeze. But in fact, it's precisely *because* we don't know them that we run into trouble.

### Unleashing the Monster

Think about it. We spend all day keeping our urges in check: not snapping at our annoying bosses, not spanking our brazen children, not admitting to our spouses that—well, yes, those jeans *do* make them look a little chubby. It requires a mountain of self-control. But we're willing to harness our impulses to keep the peace in our important relationships, not to mention our jobs.

So, occasionally, when we're dissed by complete strangers, toward whom we have no obligations at all—when they bump into us with steaming cups of coffee without so much as a sorry glance in our direction, or cut in front of us at the bank, or let the door slam closed in our faces—we're free, at last, to uncage the mighty beasts that lie within. We lose it!

At any rate, this is the best explanation I've got to explain why so many seemingly sensible people like Robert (that fellow who was second in line at Costco) are willing to throw down the gauntlet and duke it out with total strangers—over next to nothing. (And if a mad scientist injected us with sodium pentothal, wouldn't we admit that we too have suffered a few supercharged moments with irrelevant strangers?)

Well, not to worry.

Help is here, in the form of lyrics—from a pop song, no less.

### Walk On By!

You know, that sweet little chestnut from the 1960s, by Burt Bacharach and Hal David and sung by the ever-classy Dionne Warwick (before the Psychic Friends years and her daffy turn on *Celebrity Apprentice* anyway).

> *If you see me walking down the street,*
> *And I start to cry each time we meet,*
> *Walk on by, walk on by.*

That's right: Do not tangle with strangers on the street, or at the bank, or in line at Starbucks. Just walk on by.

Unlike the troubles that befall us while riding public transportation—when we're trapped underground, or in the sky, or on a crowded crosstown bus—interactions with strangers on the street have a built-in escape valve: You simply walk away!

In the internal struggle between fight and flight—and we all know the lure of a catfight—always flee, every time!

For instance:

I walk everywhere, and I'm never on my BlackBerry or cell phone. This means that I'm always moving and shifting and trying to avoid bumping into people who are looking at their phones, instead of where they're going, and start veering toward me. I want to yell at these people, "Pay attention, douche bag!" Can I tell them to get out of my way?

—*Jack, New York City*

Is this guy saying what I think he's saying? That he's not in demand, 24-7, like everyone else in the country over the age of twelve, sending and receiving e-mails, texts, and tweets every second of the day?

Fortunately, Bacharach and David—well, okay, a supremely untalented imitator—have contemplated this one:

> *If you see me walking down the street,*
> *And I start to tweet,*
> *Knocking you off your feet,*
> *Just walk on by.*

Prescient, weren't they? Cell technology didn't even exist in the mid-1960s! What's more, it's the right approach. Because as reasonable as it may be to ask strangers to watch where they're going as they lurch toward you, you'll probably be even more annoyed when you see them roll their eyes at you in response. Hate to tell you, but typing on the street has become a basic human right.

Snappy comebacks are even worse: They always end up sounding so much angrier than we mean them to, especially with strangers.

So, as annoying as it is, our best alternative on mean sidewalks is to keep our eyes peeled—like we learned to do in those Defensive Driving classes—and, yes, walk on by.

Let's try another:

I was heading out the door of my local bakery one morning, completely lost in thought. It turned out that a lady had opened the door for me, and I failed to register her kind gesture. When I turned back to thank her, she curtly said, "You're welcome," before I could open my mouth. What do you make of interactions like this?

—*Sandra, Vermont*

Hmm. Well, I hope the witch was getting decaf. I'd always assumed that this preemptive "you're welcome" required a much busier—and ruder—setting than the sleepy Maple Syrup state, but I guess it thrives wherever finger-waggers reside. Small world, isn't it?

But again, Burt and Hal have already weighed in: Walk on by, *please*, walk on by.

Silence is even more golden with a snappish sort of stranger. A comeback will almost certainly invite an escalated response from our "you're welcome" queen. And the next thing you know, you've got a Seven Years' War on your hands. Is that what you want at nine o'clock in the morning?

In fairness, Madam Door-Holder was probably really upset because her husband or boss (and most definitely her kids) don't appreciate all the nice things she does for them in the course of a day. This has nothing to do with poor Sandra, of course, who merely walked out of a bakery one morning, a little less attentive than she might have been. But as a stranger, she's an easy target for this woman's rage.

Don't engage it. Just bob and weave, and yes, Sandra—walk on by.

(And if you simply can't help yourself when one of these "you're welcome" crabs fires on you, just draw yourself up in your grandest Prince Albert of Monaco impersonation, and say, "I'd assumed as much." Then run!)

One more?

One of the biggest surprises of becoming pregnant is that practically every Tom, Dick, and Mary feels entitled to comment on my gigantic belly and actually touch it. Even strangers on the street! I hate it. What should I do?

—*Sarah, Chapel Hill, NC*

Unfortunately, these strangers are as well-meaning as they are grossly inappropriate. So, screaming to high heaven is probably not an option. Still, who wants to be thumped like a cantaloupe at the green grocers?

If she's willing to seem a little grinchy, Sarah could always extend a preventive hand and say (preferably with a smile), "I'd rather you didn't." But that seems like a lot of trouble to go through, especially if these tummy pats happen three thousand times a day. (And I'm beginning to understand why pregnant women used to sequester themselves in the olden days.)

So, the best solution is probably a Dionne-with-a-twist: "Walk on by"—with eyes averted. Refusing eye contact is the best way to avoid interactions with strangers. I know it's unfair—and puts the onus on the victim (in this case, the poor pregnant woman) to be free from unwanted tangling, but I didn't invent the world. I'm only trying to get you through it. And it's only for a few more months, right?

Okay, last one.

This time, come up with the answer on your own before reading mine. And remember, WWDD? (What would Dionne do?)

Am I wrong to blanch in bookstores and coffee shops when strangers ask me to mind their bags and laptops while they step away? If I tell them I'm uncomfortable assuming responsibility for their things, they're offended. And often, the favor is just an opening for further conversation, which I want to avoid. What should I do?

—*Mia, Los Angeles*

Well, blanching seems a bit much, Blanche. Annoyed? Sure. Blood rushing from your face? Not so much.

Many times, these folks just want to nip into the restroom or buy another scone without lugging their stuff or losing their seats. It doesn't bother me, as it affords an excellent opportunity to rifle through their bags. But if minding a laptop feels like too much responsibility, or unleashes a chatty Pandora from her box, just say, "Gosh, I was about to leave myself." There will, of course, be icy glares and stony silence when your neighbor returns and finds you still there, but that's sort of what you wanted in the first place, right?

### When *You're* the Strange Stranger

A while back, I was racing to a meeting that seemed critically important at the time. (It wasn't, of course, but that's for another chapter: Why the events we think will be huge rarely turn out to be.)

I was roaring down the street and realized that I'd left the meeting address (and my BlackBerry) at home. With no place left to turn, I rushed into Starbucks and approached a pleasant-looking woman, who was working on her laptop. Without thinking much (obviously), I convinced myself that she wouldn't mind letting me use her laptop for

Q People come up to me, almost daily, to tell me that I look like a certain celebrity: "Has anyone ever told you that you look like . . . ? " The honest answer is, "All the time!" But this celebrity is universally regarded as gorgeous, and my humble midwestern roots make me hesitant to admit the truth. What should I say?

—*Erin, Chicago*

A You're being too hard on yourself, Erin. It's not your fault you look like Joan Rivers!

Next time some stranger plays the "has anyone ever told you?" game, answer truthfully, with a dash of self-deprecation. (People love that in a hottie.) Say, "Yes, they do, but you know, I've never *once* been offered a week at Caesars Palace."

a second. "May I . . . ? " I began, then stopped as soon as I clocked her horrified expression.

Sometimes we're the freak where absolute strangers are concerned—no two ways about it. And when we are, cleave unto Dionne even tighter: Don't try to explain it away. And for God's sake, don't smile too much. (It's creepy when strangers start smiling like jack-o'-lanterns: *Halloween 12,* much?)

Just apologize and walk away—fast!

# 6

· · · · · · · · ·

# Car(tastrophes)

*See the USA in Your Own Damn Chevrolet*

Q I went camping with five friends, three to a car, one of which was mine. On the way home, I got a flat tire and couldn't find an auto shop to replace it. I was able to miss work the next day, but my car mates could not. So five drove home in one car, and I rented a hotel room for the night. Shouldn't my passengers have split the cost of the new tire and hotel with me?

—*Andi, Baltimore*

A You see, this is why I'm wary of wilderness vacations. If it's not rednecks in cutoff shirts, frisking in the forests of *Deliverance*, it's broken-down cars on deserted country roads. This would not have happened if you'd cabbed it to the Four Seasons.

Your passengers do not have to chip in for the new tire or your hotel room merely because they were passengers. On that theory, your friends are lucky your boyfriend didn't propose to you on the drive—or they'd be required to pay for the wedding reception.

This one merely requires some social fakery. "Need any money for the tire or hotel?" they might ask, scarcely hiding their desire to race off in the other car. Whereupon you reply, "Don't worry about it."

Chipping in for gasoline? Absolutely. Forking over for a new fan belt? Not so much.

Cars are stand-ins for cash.

This was a revelation to me. I thought cars were for getting to work and picking up the kids from school. But that was before the four-door Social Q's started rolling in:

I pick up my co-worker at 7:00 a.m. every day and drive her to and from work.

This can't end well. At seven o'clock in the morning, all I want are a good cup of coffee and complete silence. So the passenger must be a Chatty Cathy, or maybe singing along with the radio, right?

Wrong! Read on:

But has she ever offered to chip in for gas?

Nope. Sheila Shotgun has to be *asked* to pay up, rather than contributing her gas money voluntarily. So, what started as a fun car pool, for the car's owner, has turned into a fever pitch of fury—over gas money. And there you have it in a nutshell: Car troubles = money troubles.

Here's another:

My wife and I subscribe, with another couple, to a season of con‑certs by the Philadelphia Orchestra. On each occasion, we drive twenty minutes from our home in the suburbs to theirs, pick them up, drive them to the concert hall, and afterward, drive them home again.

Any predictions about what the trouble might be? Perhaps all the driving our poor suburban couple has to do? Nope. Or the seemingly one-way nature of this chauffeur-driven relationship? Not at all.

Read on:

The other couple is scrupulous about paying one-half of the park‑ing costs; but since we do all the driving, shouldn't they pay the entire parking fee?

Another car, another greenback. Trust me, when the problem is auto-related, the issue involves money.

### Tip No. 1: Passengers, Keep Your Wallets Open

Whenever you are sitting in the passenger seat of a car, no matter how much the owners may be smiling and chatting and singing along with the radio, they are also calculating—down to the penny—how much you owe them for the privilege of riding along.

Don't forget it, and don't be a cheapskate either. Keep that cash flowing: for gasoline, tolls, and parking, even the occasional Slurpee from the 7-Eleven. It doesn't take much—and sometimes the offer alone suffices—to let the drivers know how much you appreciate the ride. Here's a corollary:

### Tip No. 2: Don't Just Sit There, Owners.
### Ask for a Contribution Before Your Head Explodes.

There's a twist, of course. But since we're talking about cars, rest assured that it still involves money:

### Tip No. 3: It's the Driver Who Does the Damage

For instance:

My brother needed a large cash loan, and the banks were closing in twenty minutes. Since he was visiting from out of town, I drove (like a madwoman) to make it to the bank in time. In my haste, I scraped my car's front end and cracked the parking light. My brother never said a word about the damage. Shouldn't he pay for the car repairs, considering I never would have been on the road had it not been for the loan and the need to get him to the bank quickly?

—*Suzy, New York*

Save it, Sob-Story Sue! Unless your brother had a gun to your head—or was screaming at you to burn rubber in the parking lot— the damages are on you. (In fact, even if he *was* egging you on, you're still responsible.) You're a sensible adult and voluntarily took the wheel of a car.

We can appreciate that she was doing her brother a favor. But we're responsible for our own actions. If Suzy wants to blame someone, I suggest pinning this on her parents. If they hadn't conceived her brother, he wouldn't be around to ask for the loan—or necessitate a Mario Andretti impersonation.

Sorry, but that's the way it is: You break it, you bought it! Same with the following:

I borrowed a car and wrecked it. But the owner [insert one of the following]:

a. has insurance.
b. was sitting right there in the passenger seat.
c. is a really mean person.
d. cheated on me while we were married.

Am I really responsible?

Yep. You're really responsible, in every last instance. When you take the keys to someone else's car, the money to repair the damage you cause will come from your pocket. So be careful about borrowing cars—and trying to wriggle out of your responsibilities too. It just makes you look like a creep and a whiner.

Okay, big finale:

Q A friend and I hopped into a third friend's car. Neither of us wanted to drive, but he was hungover, so I agreed to. (It's also worth noting that he was staying with me at my parents' ski house.) We both missed a large No Parking sign; and when we returned from shopping, we found a boot on the car. I asked my friend to split the $120 ticket with me; neither of us did anything to avoid the situation. But he refused, saying that as the driver, I assumed the responsibilities of the road. Who's right?

—*Zeke, Boulder, CO*

Now, keep in mind the Three Principles of the Auto Zone:

1. Passengers, keep your wallets open.
2. Don't just sit there, owners. Ask for a contribution before your head explodes.
3. It's the driver who does the damage.

And here's a wild card: Where friends are concerned, split the difference wherever possible. When you've worked out an answer for Zeke in Boulder, turn the page to take a look at mine.

I think I saw a *Law & Order* like this, Zeke, except instead of illegal parking, the duo pulled an armed robbery, but the guy in the passenger seat didn't know his buddy was packing.

Technically, of course, your friend is right. State troopers don't ticket passengers for their friends' excesses behind the wheel—which is good news for Lindsay Lohan's posse. And if you had mowed someone down in the parking lot, no ambulance chaser would be suing your crony in state court.

Still, given your pal's vacation-home freeloading, the fact that neither of you wanted to drive—and frankly, your direct request for financial aid—I probably would have split the cost of the ticket with you. (Haven't we all wasted $60 in far sillier ways?) But since your friend decided not to go that route, just think of it as knowing the limits of his mensch-iosity and try not to hold it against him.

# PART 3

. . . . . . . . . . . . . . . . . . . . . . . . . . . . . . . . . . . . . . . . . . . . . . . .

# Getting Down to Business

# "Who's the Boss?"

*Handling Yours Like They Do on TV*

Q An after-work happy hour turns boozier than expected, and before I know it, I've launched into a full-on make-out session with the boss—right in front of everyone. How do I handle this at work in the morning?

—*Jane, Cincinnati*

A If you've got any ties to the Gambino crime family, now may be the perfect time for contacting the FBI. You can slip into the Witness Protection Program and off to some (really) remote place where your barroom smooching is not yet the talk of the town.

Otherwise, ride this one out. And do it John Wayne–style: Never explain, and never apologize—except to your boss, to whom you say (in ten seconds or less), "Sorry about last night.

The booze got the better of me. It won't happen again." (And if, by chance, you're a married politician or world-famous sports star, you may want to contact *60 Minutes* to schedule your televised apology to the nation.)

Have faith, Jane: Memories of your floor show will fade as soon as one of your colleagues does something equally idiotic. So, fingers crossed! And on the bright side: At least you don't work for Trump Enterprises—in which case, you'd have been locking lips with The Donald.

I love a theme song.

*"Who can turn the world on with her smile?"*

Remember that one?

*"Who can take a nothing day, and suddenly make it all seem worthwhile?"*

Well, if you grew up on it, like I did—or otherwise walked the earth during the 1970s—you already know that it's the theme from *The Mary Tyler Moore Show*, the mother of all workplace sitcoms. It aired on Saturday nights, nestled inside the most brilliant stretch of TV programming ever: *All in the Family* at eight, *The Jeffersons* at eight thirty, then *Mary Tyler Moore*, followed by *The Bob Newhart Show* at nine thirty, and culminating with *The Carol Burnett Show* at ten (which was past my bedtime, unless we had a sitter). It was the definition of appointment television.

But even if you never saw *Mary Tyler Moore*, about a single girl working at a local TV news station in Minneapolis—or can't even picture its opening sequence, with a freeze-framed image of Mary tossing her blue striped tam into a bright blue sky—you've felt its impact anyway. Because *The Mary Tyler Moore Show* was one of the first sitcoms to explore the "family dynamics" of the workplace.

You know, how Mary's gruff-but-tenderhearted boss, Lou Grant, was like a gruff-but-tenderhearted father to her; and how Murray, the sarcastic news writer, was just like her smart-aleck brother; and how Mary herself became a patient mommy to the station's dim-witted anchorman, Ted Baxter.

This approach to the workplace—as if Human Resources hired from a single gene pool—made the comedy (and conflicts) of the show feel fresh but familiar: as if our own skirmishes with parents and siblings were taking place in an office somewhere in the Midwest.

And a TV genre was born: the "office family," in which workers relate to each other more like family members than like folks who merely turn up at the same place from nine to five.

*I'm telling Mom—I mean, the boss!*

Thanks to *Mary Tyler Moore*, we (and subsequent generations of TV producers) have come to see the workplace in a rich new light, perfect for mining family-based comedy from work settings.

THE MARY TYLER MOORE SHOW
THE MARY TYLER MOORE SHOW

O                i

bROTHER         S

H           fATHER

E           E

R           R

THE MARY TYLER MOORE SHOW
THE MARY TYLER MOORE SHOW

### Solving Your Beef with the Boss Like They Do on TV:
### Just Treat 'Em Like the Father (or Mother)
### Figures They Are!

Like the best inventions, casting our bosses as parental stand-ins seems pretty obvious now. Who else has the kind of authority over us that can make us feel as helpless as a kid again? "I need it by Monday morning!" when barked by the boss on Friday afternoon, isn't much different from "You're grounded!" back when we were sixteen, right? (In fact, bosses are like parent figures from a particular time in our lives: *before* we dared to be "fresh," as my mother puts it, or rolled our eyes at them, or stormed out of the room. In short, before we learned that parents have to take our nonsense because they're—well, our parents.)

And just as there are all kinds of parents, so, too, are there all kinds of bosses, from strictly totalitarian to utterly permissive. But no matter which type of boss/parent we have, the central tenet of dealing with them is pretty consistent: Defer, where possible. Not because we agree with them, or submit to their wise authority, but because it's easier that way.

Think about it: The only thing that frees us from the "tyranny" of our parents (aside from trust funds and Lotto jackpots) is the independence-making paycheck—and the bosses who hand them to us. And if we want those paychecks, what do we do? You got it: We submit to their authority, and complain about them endlessly to others.

And when it comes to solving our problems with the boss, how best to find a creative solution? Easy!

By comparing our bosses to the ones we all share: our favorite TV bosses. Not only will this take the sting out of the situation, by helping us to remember that everyone has troubles with their boss, but it may also spur us to think as creatively as our sitcom counterparts.

Let's take a look:

My boss tells me EVERYTHING about his love life. He's a super-nice guy, and I'm happy he's found a girlfriend and all, but spending hours in his office—or worse, on the phone—hearing about his new flame (and their spats, and their sex life) is wearing thin. I've got work to do, and he won't take the hint. How can I get him to shut up about her?

Three little words: "Monster dot com!"

Hmm. The oversharing boss: Sound anything like Mr. Peterman, Elaine's yarn-spinning employer on *Seinfeld*—the one who regaled her with stories of lusty nights atop Machu Picchu or making out in the Mekong Delta, and whose company sold ridiculous clothing inspired by his far-flung adventures ("Urban Sombrero," anyone?). Or how about Steve Carell's Michael Scott, the dimwitted manager of the Scranton branch of Dunder Mifflin from *The Office*, who never met a sexual moment he didn't force his employees to squirm through?

Well, this "and one more thing about my new girlfriend" boss is just like them. And as with his sitcom doppelgängers, I'm going to assume that simple requests, like "She sounds great, but I better get back to work," sail right over his head. Then what can you do—storm out in a huff? I think not.

Unfortunately, our paychecks prevent us from pulling the plug on conversations that our self-absorbed bosses really want to have. And a ready supply of topic-changers only works from time to time.

The only alternative, I'm afraid, is to get as creative as they do on TV: Get your boss to go away by becoming even more involved with him—temporarily anyway. Invite the oversharing boss to dinner, and make sure he brings his new gal pal. After spending the entire evening chatting with his newfound mate, just tell your boss (when he next launches into a play-by-play of their relationship) that you don't feel comfortable talking about your new BFF behind her back.

Voilà! Unwanted confidences, banished! Until your clueless boss blows it with his girlfriend and moves on to another squeeze. What's more, it's a sitcom episode in the making, and may make you feel like a celebrity, to boot.

Here's another one:

My boss is superrich. If I tell him I bought a digital camera for $129, he tells me I should have bought the $4,000 model instead. But that's a month's pay for me—and he knows how much I earn. Still, if I tell him I went to the Jersey Shore for the weekend, he's almost guaranteed to say that he prefers the South of France. How should I deal with this guy?

Probably *not* by bashing him over the head with his 18-karat gold stapler! Mr. Filthy Rich sounds like a dreamy (sitcom) boss—that clueless mogul who owned the station on *News Radio*, for instance; or Karen, Grace's pampered assistant who ruled the design office on *Will & Grace*; or even Alec Baldwin's perk-laden Jack Donaghy on *30 Rock*.

On sitcoms, as in real life, the boss helps those who help themselves. So just point-and-click your low-rent digital camera to lock down a pay raise! Get the boss to share his goodies—or at least shut up about them—by being as direct as he is.

The next time your boss starts waxing about some luxurious bauble you could never afford, just chime in, "Gosh, I'd love an estate in the Dominican Republic! But it's going to be hard to swing on my current salary. How about a 10 percent pay raise?"

Your prospects are twofold: Either the silly bragging boss gives you the raise (not so likely), or your request adds a chaffing discomfort to his swagger and may cause him to dial it back a little. (But you never know: You may just find a few dollars more in your next paycheck—or a Maserati in your driveway, courtesy of the man in charge.)

Okay, one more:

I'm a hardworking young guy in the fashion business who is occasionally five minutes late getting to work in the morning. My boss has made it clear that this is one of her pet peeves. But what difference does it make, in the grand scheme of things, if I'm a few minutes late? When I arrive I get right to work, rather than spending half an hour making breakfast and talking about my personal life, like my on-time colleagues. I also stay later than everyone else. How can I tell her that I'm right?

You are absolutely right, young man! In the "grand scheme of things," it matters not a whit that you are five minutes late. But what in hell makes you think your job has anything to do with the grand scheme of things?

This sounds like a job for Bob Newhart, the 1970s TV shrink, whose smart-aleck secretary walked all over him, or Candice Bergen on *Murphy Brown,* whose inability to keep an assistant for more than thirty minutes was a running gag for the length of the show. Or maybe those hapless interns on *Scrubs,* who always managed to learn something about life in each slapstick-laden, slightly saccharine episode?

Because when you're wrong, latecomer, you're wrong! I hate to break it to you, but our bosses are—well, the boss of us, during work hours anyway (and assuming sexual favors have not been requested). While some bosses are prepared to let stragglers slide, in exchange for late departures or better output, others don't see it that way.

Try not to lose sleep over the injustice of it all. The issue is much simpler: How much of Lady Boss's goodwill are you prepared to burn over this? For your sake, I hope the answer is "not much." Otherwise, you're in for a long slog of workplace battles that are much better finessed. So no more punching the Snooze button, okay?

### When Sitcoms Aren't Enough

Hard as this may be to believe, sometimes in life we come upon a problem (or three) for which sitcoms are not equipped to help us:

*My boss has a habit of leering at my breasts and letting his hands brush my backside when we pass in the hallways. I feel really uncomfortable with him.*

Or:

*My boss includes me on group e-mails that are racist and really of-fensive. Since I'm a member of a racial minority myself, I'm thinking this must be a mistake.*

What to do then?

Well, it's a safe bet that we've moved out of *Mary Tyler Moore* terri-tory. Sometimes a simple "No" will suffice to an unwanted touching, or "You must have meant this for someone else" in response to a bigoted e-mail.

But even though I generally counsel deference where bosses are concerned—in fact, "smarmy suck-up" is my ATM password—don't let yourself become the victim of a bad boss. It's damaging to your mo-rale and can harm your career. So confide in a friend or make the dreaded trip to Human Resources, and strategize your way out of the situation. Trust me, no one wants a creep around, and if you're able to flag the problem discreetly—without subjecting yourself to retaliation—go for it.

Annoying bosses are one thing, and clueless bosses are another, but when they begin to infringe on our basic rights and dignity, it's not a laughing matter anymore. So deal with the problem or start looking for another job (or both).

Now that you've got the idea, let's see if you can handle the following problem—the sitcom way. Just project yourself onto the cast of your favorite workplace sitcom and figure out how to handle this boss:

Q I just started a job as an administrative assistant, writing and proofreading sales materials that we send to clients. I have a BA in English and lots of confidence in my abilities. Still, whenever it comes time to write a letter, my boss asks his wife to do it instead of me. (She has no affiliation with the company.) I feel mildly insulted that he relies on her for tasks that I'm qualified to do myself. How should I resolve this?

Got a sitcom in mind? Or a favorite sitcom employee? Here's a hint: Think of a career girl who's new to the big, bad city of Minneapolis and dying to become a producer of TV news segments.

You got it! Circle back to Mary Richards on *The Mary Tyler Moore Show* and give it a whirl. How will she ever get Lou to let her write that letter?

What a work ethic! Most of us are trying to figure out how to shirk our responsibilities, not take on more.

Happily, there's a quick-and-dirty solution, as well as a more labor-intensive one: Just tell your boss that his wife is having an affair with her personal trainer. Those letters should fall right into your lap once they're legally separated!

Or you can prove yourself in your new job, and earn your boss's trust the traditional way—over time. Think about it: He's been relying on his wife's good counsel for years, while you've just arrived on the scene. Let him see you in action; show him you're an asset to the firm. Then say politely, "I'd like to take a crack at that letter if you wouldn't mind."

I'll bet he says yes. If not, revert to Plan A. But make sure to have the names of a few good divorce lawyers handy in case your boss needs them.

# 8

· · · · · · · · ·

# Taking the "Woe" out of Co-Workers

*Just Because You Sit Together Doesn't Make You Besties*

Q My name is James. I introduce myself as James and sign my name as James. But my co-workers always refer to me as "Jimmy." I think the nickname conveys an image of immaturity, and is inappropriate with clients and other professionals. How do I get my colleagues to change the way they refer to me?

—James, Long Island, NY

A Have you thought about wearing long pants to the office, and maybe leaving that little red wagon at home?

People who christen us with nicknames, on their own steam, think they're being "regular," and respond poorly to statements like "Please call me by my full name." They see their nicknaming as a hearty gesture of friendliness, and take our correction as stuck-up.

Here's what you do: Simply repeat your name (in full) as

often as possible. If your boss introduces you to a new client, "This is Jimmy," you'll say, "It's James" when you shake her hand. Answer your telephone: "This is James." Repetition is the key. That way, you're not correcting anyone or acting snooty, just reinforcing your desired result.

If that doesn't work, choose a new nickname that conveys the professionalism you're after. (People love to get in on a new nickname.) How would you feel about Spike?

Despite what your mother may have told you and your siblings, everyone has favorites—even her. I know I do. There's full-fat chocolate ice cream; those Acne jeans I got on sale at Barneys; and my best friend, Chiccio. They're my top draft picks, simple as that.

Of course, there are many other things in this world that I'm perfectly fond of, especially when my favorites aren't readily available. Weight Watchers fudgesicles, for instance, if we're out of Ben & Jerry's, the jeans I wore before the Acne jeans (if my favorites are in the laundry hamper), and the pals I call when my besties are busy or out of town. These other things are perfectly fine, just not my faves.

Like versus love: not a hard concept, right?

So keep it in mind, because this distinction is going to come in handy when we consider the conflicts that tend to arise between co-workers. The most common troubles in the workplace (or the ones that most commonly find their way to Social Q's anyway) come from the failure to distinguish between co-workers (whom we like perfectly well) and bona fide friends (whom we actually love).

Think about it: Just because we sit next to someone for eight hours a day—a person, by the way, who was assigned to sit there by our employer—does that make him or her an intimate? Of course not!

It makes them someone we should treat respectfully, but not necessarily someone with whom we should share our marital troubles—or worse, someone whose marital troubles we should take it upon ourselves to diagnose, dispensing unbidden advice as we would with family members or close friends.

*I don't think your boyfriend is good enough for you,* for example.

Step back! Before you weigh in on your co-worker's love life, tell me this: Is she someone you actually care about, or are you just passing the time with her because your real pals are sitting in their own offices across town?

Like versus love, remember?

It's an understandable error. We're often bored at work, and we're social animals at heart, so we delude ourselves occasionally into thinking that we're "close" with that woman in the next cubicle. We confuse physical proximity with emotional intimacy. And sometimes, if our favorite people aren't around, we can actually convince ourselves that we're crazy about folks we barely like. (I can't be the only one who's wolfed down an entire box of Mallomars—mostly because they were there—only to realize that I didn't even like them, can I?)

Well, it's the same with work pals. Do we really like them, or do we just like them because they're there? And if it's the latter, better to back off and not become too embroiled in their lives (or they in ours).

Because here's the thing: Work friendships are largely geographical in nature. If we didn't have adjoining cubicles, we'd never know most of our co-workers. And the proof of this is once we leave the company, we rarely speak with them again. Or if we do, it's strained and uncomfortable, and we wonder how we were ever so close. So try to keep this in mind—she's the friendly gal at work, not your best friend—and watch your troubles melt away.

Let's start with an easy one:

A guy that I work with—who seems very nice, but whom I don't really know—has a habit of keeping his shirt unbuttoned down to, um, there. His ample chest fluff is the first thing that greets anyone who sees him at any point during the day. How can I get him to button up?

Your company doesn't have a "manscaping" department, by any chance, does it? (Too bad.)

So, what kind of person is this Tom Selleck at the next desk over? Let me give you a clue: He *seems* nice, but we *don't really know.* We're pretty much strangers who happen to work at the same place. So why in the name of Harry Larry would we tell this fellow how to tend his garden? Are you in the habit of approaching strangers on the street to critique their wardrobes? Just because you receive a paycheck signed by the same guy doesn't make you any better acquainted.

Don't get me wrong: It's better not to be distracting at the office—in what we wear or, more precisely, what we don't wear. And shirts unbuttoned to the navel, whether on men or women (of the smooth or hirsute variety), do exactly that. Still, this man, who missed a button (or three) is none of our concern. Better to stay out of it.

Here's another:

My best friend at the office always underpays when we go out to lunch. At first, it was just a couple of bucks, but gradually the underpayments have increased. Last time, it was nearly $15. She usually dashes out before the meal is over, leaving me and other colleagues to pick up her slack. How can we get her to pay up?

Have you thought about banging on her cubicle wall? "Hey, cheapskate, you owe me fifteen bucks!"

Now, a "best friend at the office" can mean many things, from "blood sisters" to "the person I loathe the least." But one thing is sure: This is a person toward whom we have some level of affection. What's more, we're dealing with a pretty cut-and-dried issue here—consistent underpayment of the lunch tab—which will not require any wading into psychological territory best left to our shrinks or those annoying trainers on *The Biggest Loser*.

So hop right in, but gently. Try casting the problem as an honest mistake: "I think you made a math error at lunch." Remember to show your work. I bet she takes the point—and the problem disappears as fast as that plate of fries she ordered for the table.

Let's try another:

At fifty-four, I'm the second-oldest person at the school where I work. On occasional Friday afternoons, several teachers get together for a beer at a restaurant nearby. Everybody used to be invited, but in the last couple of years, only the young people are included. I asked a couple of the organizers to let me know when they next meet. They agreed, but I've never heard from them. The rejection makes me feel bad. Any advice?

Well, I hate to break it to you, but you're probably not going to be invited to *Vanity Fair*'s Oscars party or Malia Obama's birthday dinner either. We can't all be invited to everything, and even though it stings, it's just a part of life.

For the record, I admire your asking to be included, in the first place. Most of us wouldn't have had the guts for that. But now that you've asked, and been refused, where do you go from here?

Well, nowhere. We can't be everyone's cup of tea, any more than everyone can be ours. So here's what you do: Don't ask again. For better or worse, the whippersnappers are entitled to socialize with whomever they want. These guys are not your dearest friends, who owe you more; they're just guys who teach at the same school as you.

So how about starting a new tradition instead? Invite all your colleagues—even the youthquake splinter group—for drinks on the last Friday of every month. You'll be turning the other cheek and bolstering school morale at the same time. Now, that's a solution everyone can love, right?

Okay, last one:

I recently returned to work from maternity leave and found the office drastically changed. My co-workers are really cold to me and talk about me behind my back, especially about me and an older male co-worker, who's become a mentor to me. He and I go to lunch every once in a while, and my co-workers are suggesting that we are having sex—and worse, that he's the father of my child. This is really hurting me. I work so hard and try to be a good colleague. What should I do?

Toxic co-workers! Beware!

It's easy to be mean, and unfortunately, it's breathtakingly fun on occasion, which is why we know every stupid thing that Lindsay Lohan (and her mother *and* her father) have ever done, but next to nothing about the electoral college, say, or the quantum law of physics.

For what it's worth, gossip always says more about the people trading it than it does about its victims. And my usual advice is to put it right out of your head. But not in this case. The nasty colleagues have crossed a line, and shown themselves to be malicious. Do not engage them directly. Even a calm word could be twisted out of context and fuel even more venom. I'd speak with the boss and ask for help. Speculating about the sex lives of others is never cool, and under some circumstances, can even constitute sexual harassment under the law.

Better safe than sorry: Get help!

## Co-Workers and Their Nasty Habits

### *When You Just Can't Take It for Another Second!*

You know what I mean.

*The woman who sits next to me chews like a cow. I can hear the smacking of her lips no matter where I hide. Please help!*

Or:

*The guy who sits in front of me strokes his hair ALL DAY LONG. It is driving me crazy!*

Or choose one of the following:

1.  My boss whistles until I could scream;
2.  My boss hums—off-key, mind you—until I want to die; or
3.  My boss's perfume makes me sick to my stomach. The mere sight of the ugly lavender bottle is enough to make me gag!

They're the pet peeves from hell!

What can we do about them?

It doesn't matter whether we like these folks or hate them. We've simply got to make this damned behavior stop. (Either that, or be hauled off to the nearest mental institution.)

So here's what you do. In the calmest voice possible, say, "You know, I have no right to ask, but could you stop [INSERT HIDEOUS HABIT HERE]?" Then add, with a big smile, "For some reason, it's really getting under my skin!"

It's debatable, of course, whether the person sitting next to you has the right to chomp his food like a barnyard animal. But why go there? By making believe that it's your problem—and by being charming about it, to boot—you will be much more effective in stopping it. You avoid defensiveness and even the prospect that there's something to be defensive about.

And in my experience: It works!

If you have to remind your colleagues a couple of times about knocking off the dastardly habit, that's okay. Just do it in the same sweet, blame-accepting way.

In the end, who cares—as long as it stops, right?

Okay, now that you've got the flavor of the exercise, let me give you one to solve on your own. Once you've come up with your solution, turn the page to take a look at mine.

Q When speaking English with me, a multilingual co-worker pronounces words from other languages in the full accent of the word's origin. For example, "I'm thinking of going to Barcelona (bar-theh-LO-na) for Christmas (instead of bar-seh-LO-na). Does her technically correct pronunciation trump the fact that I find it rather awkward?

—*Debbie, New York City*

Awkward? What's French for pretentious, Debbie?

This sounds like one of those super-fancy French chocolates that are too sophisticated for my Hershey-loving palate.

It would be one thing if your co-worker's native language were coloring her pronunciation. Accents are sexy; everyone knows that. But this woman seems to be giving you the "ooh-la-la" in many different tongues, as if she were auditioning to be a foreign correspondent for CNN or to do a television spot for General Mills' International Coffees. (Remember them?)

Feel free to mock her behind her back. Or if it's driving you absolutely crazy, tell her *"Basta!"* *"Arrêtez!"* or *"Shimete yo!"*—unfortunately, giving her one last chance to correct your accent while showing off hers.

# 9

. . . . . . . . .

# Free at Last!

*After You've Quit or (Let's Face It) Been Fired*

Q For three years, I worked for a supervisor without boundaries. She asked me to care for her kids and pets, told me more about her marriage than *anyone* should have to hear, and insisted that I attend her family functions. I let her behave this way because I wanted to please her (and didn't know how to get out of it). I finally left the position, but my former boss wants our "great friendship" to continue. How can I bring this relationship down about five notches—basically, to a holiday card exchange?

—*Helen, Iowa City*

A Someone didn't watch *All About Eve* very carefully.

The whole point of sucking up is to get ahead in your *current* job (or steal the starring role from Bette Davis), not to humor supervisors from days gone by. How can you walk your old boss's Labradoodle when your new one's Shih Tzu needs a bath?

Extricating yourself is a cinch: Simply plead busyness, exhaustion, or a mild case of ennui the next few times she calls. You'll be off the hook by the end of the month. Remember, she's breaking in a new assistant as we speak, so she'll have a new marriage counselor in no time.

But I'm more concerned about your current gig. Part of the reason your old boss made such a patsy of you is that you let her, or thought you had to. Not to go all Stuart Smalley on you, but when you really value the skills you bring to work, it's easier to see when requests are out of line.

So do your job with gusto and nix the boss's kiddie car pool: "Sorry, I'm too busy here with work." And when you're not sure, ask Human Resources or your office's version of Joan from *Mad Men*. She'll be the stacked one in the tight red dress.

Life hands us surprisingly few opportunities to say, "Screw it!" Between demanding spouses and needy kids, parents who need visiting and bosses who need refills, dear old friends who are in trouble and neighbors who find themselves in a pinch, we're pretty much indentured servants to the people in our lives, from the moment we wake up in the morning until we drag our tired carcasses to bed.

You know I'm right. So when life hands us a gold-plated opportunity to say, "Not my job!"—literally—why not run with it?

Then why do I receive so many questions from readers about their former bosses and colleagues? We feel too guilty, it seems, to

tell these folks to hit the high road even after we leave the jobs
(and paychecks) that bound us to them in the first place.

This would be understandable if we were talking about family businesses, where the underlying relationship persists, or situations where the need for references from these former colleagues
lives on. But generally, that's not the story. We seem to have a
wee bit of trouble saying, "Drop dead!" So repeat after me: "Drop."
Good. Now: "Dead." Better.

Take a look:

My former boss and I parted on unfriendly terms six months ago,
when I discovered that she'd slept with my husband. I recently

discovered that she's still using my voice on her office voice-mail message. I don't feel comfortable with this. How do I get my voice off that tape?

Hang on a slimy second! Your boss sleeps with your husband, and you're worried about voice mail?

Notwithstanding my concern for your priorities, your request seems eminently reasonable. So why not send an e-mail?: "Hey, sleazeball, get my voice off your answering machine."

Or charge her royalties—for your voice and your husband. Start with a million bucks and negotiate down.

Here's another one:

A former colleague is a '70s girl who took any drug offered and dropped a lot of acid. Everything was fine until she started telling me—every day—that my "body language" was cold to her and that I never asked her to lunch. It got a little much for me, so I found another job. But this woman has been in a furor ever since, calling me several times a day! I have no experience with people who used drugs to her extent. How do I deal with this?

Just say no, Mrs. Reagan! Your job is done, and so is your relationship with this crazy *former* colleague.

But on a side note: I'm no Druggy McBongwater, but neediness toward one's colleagues is not exactly a classic sign of drug abuse. And thirty years seems a bit long for a hallucinatory hangover.

So be careful about ascribing your former pal's weird behavior to drugs. You have a legitimate beef; no need to cloak it in gossip.

Just ask Madam Looney Tunes to stop calling. If she continues, report the harassment to the police. And be wary of your new co-workers: They may be high on crack.

Okay, last one—on a similar theme, but a sadder note:

> When I lost my job last year, it came as a painful shock to me. I'd always thought my friend (in Human Resources) and I were close. But I'm sure she knew about the layoff and did nothing to warn me. Recently, she's been asking me to lunch and dinner. I found another job, but I still feel hurt. I want to keep her as a reference, but no longer trust her as a friend. Please help.

It stings when colleagues hurt our feelings, but it's much worse when we consider the colleague a legitimate friend.

But the pal in HR was probably *required* by the company to keep the layoffs under wraps. That's not to diminish the hurt, or to say that she couldn't have given you a triple-secret heads-up. But she was in a bind too.

If she was really a friend, think about reconnecting. Just clear the air: "It hurt my feelings when you laid me off, and I wish you'd prepared me for it." Your friend in HR may feel terrible about this too—and we can take real comfort when friends feel our pain. But if you're really done with her, and only want her as a reference, just tell her your new job is keeping you busy, and that you look forward to seeing her when things quiet down (which should be some time after hell freezes over).

The concept is pretty easy.

The old job was "then," and this is "now." And for most of us, it's pretty clear which of our former bosses and co-workers we want in our current Rolodexes and which we want on the trash heap. So don't be afraid to assert yourself a little.

And to those unwanted colleagues, just ask, "How can I miss you if you won't go away?"

# PART 4

· · · · · · · · · · · · · · · · · · · · · · · · · · · · · · · · · · · · · · · · · · · · · · ·

# Getting Online

# Step Away from That Keyboard!

*E-mails, Texts, and the Three Commandments for E-living*

Whenever I see a cute boy—on the train or on the street—instead of boldly approaching him, I write a Craigslist ad: "Missed Connection." For the last few months, this guy has been walking by the glass storefront of the place I work. He peers in, and we often smile at each other, but neither of us has had the nerve to speak, nor has he responded to my Craigslist posting. Is a simple "hello" good enough to get things started, or do I have to be more intriguing?

—*Angela, San Francisco*

Craigslist is heaven on earth for unloading your granny's old chintz sofa, the favorite perch of her incontinent cat. It's also handy for finding local hookers and for throwing that Hail Mary pass: searching for the bewitching stranger who smiled at you as his train chugged out of the station.

But why, in the name of Steve Jobs, would you use your computer to find a guy who walks by your workplace every day of the week? Step away from your laptop, Walter Mitty!

The next time your hoped-for Romeo peeks in your window, simply head for the door and say, "Hello." Trust me, his smiling in for several months is as close to a sure thing as you're going to get in this life. And keep the banalities and awkward chatter going until you make a date or exchange information.

But so help me, young lady, if I hear that you're exchanging flirty text messages with him instead of meeting face-to-face, I'll smoke you out and dumb down your smartphone!

E-mails and texts are so freaking good at what they're good at, it's hard to imagine how busy people—like William Shakespeare or Truman Capote—ever lived without them. Is there any better way to make plans (*See you at the theater at 7:45*), establish simple facts (*When is Mom's birthday, again?*), or convey large bodies of information (*Here are seven pictures of my cheating ex-boyfriend's muffin top—from different angles and perspectives. Hope you enjoy them as much as I do!*)?

E-communication is so quick and efficient that we may be tempted to use it for everything. But that would be a huge mistake. And one that virtually all of us have made.

E-mailing your son's second-grade report card to your husband, for instance? Great idea! But sending it to every single employee at the company where you work? Not so much.

Or breaking up with your boyfriend in a clear and compassionate way? Nothing short of admirable—if an unfortunate fact of life. But doing it via text message? Put down the phone, girl-friend.

Which of us hasn't been victim (and perpetrator!) of electronic messaging run amok? In fact, the misuse of e-mail and text messaging is rampant, with inappropriate and hurtful messages multiplying faster than tacky reality shows on the Bravo network. (I'm hoping for mine any minute!)

So before falling prey to these ever-so-tempting media again, consider this simple three-part test *before* you press that Send button.

### It's as Easy as 1-2-3—or in This Case, O-M-G!

**O:** Only for easy stuff;

**M:** Make sure; and

**G:** Get on the phone at the FIRST sign of trouble.

And there you have it:

### The Three Commandments of Your Electronic Life.

Let's break it down:

### *First Commandment: O—Only for Easy Stuff*

Figuring out what's "easy" and what isn't is like Supreme Court justice Potter Stewart's definition of porn: "I know it when I see it." So, "easy" includes making dinner dates with friends, asking and answering routine questions from co-workers, scheduling meetings, and even complimenting someone: "You looked great in that red dress last night!"

Criticizing her is a different story. How about "Wow! You looked like a two-dollar hooker in that getup"? Never!

In fact, any time we need to criticize, quibble, or reject someone (and so, by definition, the message is likely to upset them or hurt their feelings), better to skip the keyboard and proceed directly to the telephone or their doorstep, regardless of how much we'd like to dispose of the matter via e-mail or text, and especially if we really want to handle it that way because we're too chicken to do it in person.

It doesn't take a rocket scientist to understand the impulse: We have something hard to say. Anyone in his right mind would jump at the chance not to say it in person.

But saying it from a safe distance doesn't make it right; it just lets you off the hook.

For instance, *I've admired you from afar for such a long time. But at last, the time feels right for asking, Will you go out with me?*

Or, *I've worked so hard as your assistant for the last two years. Isn't it time for a promotion and a raise?*

Or even, *I have the clap—so, unfortunately, you probably do too.*

Nobody likes to risk rejection, or ask for more money when it might not come, or share bad news (well, with people we care about anyway). But these hard duties are facts of life. And while the lure of the passive e-mail or text is understandable, it is not the way to go.

Why not? you ask.

Because electronic messaging diminishes the impact of the message, and depersonalizes it too. Just as e-mails and texts may shield us from feeling vulnerable when we broach a tricky subject, they also seem less heartfelt (and serious) to their recipients. In short, it puts "Will you go out with me?" on a par with "There are doughnuts in the fortieth-floor conference room!" So if you really want to persuade that guy or gal to date you, show up in person and plead your case. If you think you've earned that raise or promotion, appear before your boss and ask for it—and be prepared to explain why you deserve it.

And finally, if you have a case of venereal disease, be man or woman enough, damn it, to stand before your partner and apologize, possibly with a superdose of antibiotics in your pocket.

These folks deserve to hear it personally—from you.

### Second Commandment: M—Make Sure

The First Commandment requires a bit of judgment. Is the subject matter of our message easy or hard? Well, here's the good news: The Second Commandment requires no judgment at all!

After you've typed your e-mail or text message, STOP IN THE NAME OF NORTON ANTIVIRUS! Do not press Send, even though you may think you're finished, because you're not.

Before sending your message, make sure to:

- **Proofread.** Spelling and grammatical errors in messages can make us look like Jethro Clampett from *The Beverly Hillbillies*. What's more, mangled sentences can cause our friends and co-workers—and especially, our bosses—to think that we're mangled thinkers too. (And we know that we're geniuses just waiting to be discovered, right?) So take a minute to tidy up.

- **Eliminate** (1) ridiculous abbreviations ("u" for "you"); (2) emoticons (death to ☺, at least until they come up with a smirking face we can use in reply, preferably caught in the act of spitting in disgust); and (3) alphanumeric lameness ("gr8!"). All of these devices are fantastic if you're in middle school; otherwise, they make us look like pathetic adults still pining for our *Gossip Girl* years. ☹

- **Remove extraneous Cc's.** Believe it or not, very few of the folks in our address books actually want to see that photo album of the family outing to Splish Splash, especially coming so close on the heels of those thrilling pictures we circulated of our bathroom renovation. The same goes for that brilliant memo we wrote on Supply Chain Management. Spend a minute to confirm that every addressee might really want (or need) to see our message. (And this goes double before sending sensitive financial information—annual bonus lists or the ten hottest rich guys we know!) Pare down your recipients to the bare minimum. You'll save yourself from being the subject of a lot of eye-rolling that way.

- **Wait** two hours, at least, before sending a message that is angry, snippy, or sarcastic. Let it simmer for a while first. And if you still feel committed to sending it after a reasonable waiting period—and you are not currently enrolled in a court-ordered anger management class—then let it rip. But be warned: Sending an angry message is probably a mistake. Here's the thing—e-mails don't have facial expressions (save the dreaded emoticon) or tones of voice, and a snippy message, in plain black and white, can seem furious when it appears in an inbox; an angry one can seem downright nuclear! (The same goes for sarcastic humor: It's often misinterpreted on the page.) So be careful, and try to avoid these messages whenever possible.

### Third Commandment: G—Get on the Phone
### (or Their Doorstep) at the FIRST Sign of Trouble

Now, if you couldn't take my advice about avoiding angry messages—or if you receive an unsolicited, electronic slap across the face, or find yourself in the midst of an escalating e-mail misunderstanding or text message brouhaha—beware! Continued e-mails and text messages are rarely your friends in such scenarios.

For instance:

I'm throwing my parents a surprise twenty-fifth-anniversary party. I want to invite all their friends and family members, so it's getting to be expensive. I e-mailed my brother to ask him for a contribution. He's kind of broke, so I didn't ask for half the costs, only a quarter of them. He sent me back a really mean text, accusing me of calling him cheap, which I never did. (Though he is!) I sent back an e-mail telling him he was crazy, and that I only asked for a quarter of the costs because I know he's poor and didn't want to embarrass him. Now he won't return my texts or e-mails. The party is getting close. What should I do?

Three words of advice: Stop. The. Madness.

Sister Woman needs to log out of Gmail and call her brother on the telephone, or visit his broke ass (in his undoubtedly dumpy little apartment). Her brother has somehow gotten the wrong idea about her request for a contribution. (We'll just pretend she didn't include that nasty parenthetical about his being cheap.) Chances are, a two-minute phone call will straighten out this whole business, bringing a peaceful end to the War of the Twenty-Fifth Anniversary before the really heavy artillery is launched. ("Mom always liked you better!")

The same goes for the rest of us.

At the first sign of trouble—or misunderstanding, or full-on catfight—step away from your laptop (or BlackBerry) and call the other guy on the phone. All I am saying, in the words of John Lennon, "is give peace a chance." And the fact is, it's virtually impossible to reroute a poisonous electronic exchange electronically. That requires the human touch.

Don't get me wrong: It can be a rush to channel our meanest selves in e-mail warfare. There's something about the anonymity of a blank computer screen that lulls us into typing horrible things that we would *never* say to a person's face. (I've done it myself more than a few times!) But here's the thing to remember: An actual person is going to open that e-mail and read every nasty word of that message. And then it's not so fun anymore, is it?

So tamp down your warrior impulse before launching that hostile message. And if your pal (or sibling or co-worker) slips, and fires the first missile, sending a nasty e-mail or text your way, be the bigger person—and delete it. Then march to the phone and talk it out. You'll be amazed at how quickly we can work most problems out.

Now that you know the Three Commandments of Electronic Messaging by that well-known mnemonic—OMG!—let's look at a few examples.

Remember:

**O:** Only for easy stuff;
**M:** Make sure; and
**G:** Get on the phone at the FIRST sign of trouble.

I recently learned that a former colleague, with whom I used to be friendly but haven't seen in years, lost her son to suicide last year. I want to send my condolences. I was going to send an e-mail message, but maybe this sort of thing should be done over the phone or in a handwritten note?

First off, it's great that you're going to get in touch with your friend. She can probably use your support, and many people might hide behind the length of time that's lapsed since you've been friendly and let it slide.

It probably doesn't matter much *how* you contact her, but here's my preference: A phone call (out of the blue, on a painful subject) forces your pal to respond on the spot, whether she wants to or not. Written communication gives her more control; she can respond when she's ready. And it also gives her a memento of your kindness that she can refer back to later.

An e-mail message doesn't feel quite right to me either—sandwiched in her inbox between her cell phone bill and that YouTube clip of a kitten on a trampoline. So I'm going to invoke the First Commandment, "O: Only for easy stuff," and suggest you avoid an e-mail or text.

Go with a handwritten note.

Let's try another:

A friend of mine recently sent a mass e-mail declaring that he could be silent no more about his wife's many accomplishments. He went on, at great length, about her many charitable qualities—likening her to both Jesus and Gandhi. He then asked that we send her a congratulatory message. Is this as crazy as I think?

Well, this much is clear: The letter writer is a good person. Most people I know would have circulated the husband's message so widely that the sheer volume of cackling, in reply, would have driven the clueless husband and his goody-two-shoes wife into the mountains of Afghanistan, where, presumably, Mrs. Jesus would have captured every last one of Osama bin Laden's cronies and brought them peaceably to justice.

Since you avoided the public humiliation route, I'd file this under "M: Make sure." Just delete Hubby's message and cut him some slack. God knows, we've all made mistakes with e-mail. No need to rub his nose in it. It sounds as if your friend may have been drunk when he wrote this, or trying really hard to make up to his wife for some other boneheaded stunt.

If these messages continue, hit the "spam" button faster than if he were trying to sell you a penis-enlargement cream!

Okay, last one:

A good friend's husband is running for political office. I don't live in their district, but I donated to his campaign anyway. My friend sent me a text message, chastising me for not making a bigger gift and requesting another. I politely declined, by return text, and she sent me an angry message, detailing my contributions to other campaigns and demanding an explanation. What should I do?

Down, political pit bull! Down! If the wife in question weren't a good friend, I'd advise doing nothing. The letter writer didn't owe her an explanation after the first message, and she really doesn't owe her one after the second. But since she is a good

### Don't Make Me Take That Phone Away from You!

#### *Phones and BlackBerries at Dinner, on Dates, and at Meetings*

We all know the lure of a vibrating phone. How can we possibly stop ourselves from peeking at that new e-mail or text?

I don't know—but you've got to. Really.

Nothing feels worse than sitting at the table with a friend, date, or colleague while he checks his phone ad nauseam instead of paying attention to us, right? Well, it's just as bad when we do it—and not cool. So don't!

Here's my trick: Turn your phone to silent mode when the person you're meeting first pops into view, then stow it in your pocket. That way, you'll receive the message that your pal is running late, but won't be tempted by every successive buzz for the length of your meeting.

I know it's hard, but you can do it. Think of it like the buildup to Christmas morning. When the meal is over, just think how many text messages you'll find underneath the tree!

If there's something critical brewing at the office—which, in reality, happens once every year or so—apologize in advance for checking your Crackberry every twenty minutes. (Note: I didn't say every ninety seconds, did I?) And if that emergency really comes to pass, then respond quickly, mute your phone, and behave as detailed above. And don't even think of replying to any of the other messages, even though I know you're dying to!

friend, go with the Third Commandment: "G: Get on the phone at the FIRST sign of trouble."

Call her up and let her know that you sympathize with how hard it must be to be at the center of the political dogfight, and that you've given what you feel comfortable giving. Period.

Let's hope your pal sees the error of her ways sometime after the general election.

Now, occasionally, I receive word from some poor soul who actually misses chatting on the phone with colleagues and friends:

> Lately I've noticed that every time I leave a voice message asking for someone to call me back—co-workers, my kids, even my lawyer—the response comes in the form of an e-mail or a text message. Is there anything I can do about this? All this typewritten text feels so impersonal to me.

Can you imagine?

Well, at this point, asking people to step away from their keyboards is a little like asking the Kardashian girls to be more like Audrey Hepburn. That ship has sailed. Still, I applaud the impulse: wanting to know pals and colleagues as people, instead of merely as typists.

Here's what you do: Be more like e-mail!

People like e-mails and texts because they can deal with them when they like. So never call first thing in the morning (when there are bagels to be toasted) or at the end of the day (when hasty retreats are in the offing). I suggest the window between 11:00 a.m. and 4:00 p.m.

The best e-mails are brief. So don't natter endlessly either. The people on the other end of the phone might be preparing for their annual review or updating their Match.com profile.

And never try to out-e-mail an e-mail: A phone call will never substitute for describing that clip on YouTube. Just attach and send.

People may still resist your calls. But you never know. If you're persistent and charmingly offbeat, you may just inspire one or two to dial you back!

Okay, last one:

Q I was visiting a friend in the mountains, who suggested that we go for a walk in a nearby national park to pick wildflowers. I told her that I'd love to go for a walk, but that picking wildflowers wasn't right, because it prevents the flowers from setting seed for the next year. We went for a walk; she picked her flowers, and I said nothing. Later she posted on her Facebook page (and her blog) that she'd been out with the "Nature Gestapo"! She encouraged others to follow her example and ignore my prudish advice. After my visit, I sent her an e-mail, telling her that her posts hurt my feelings. We haven't spoken since. Is this friendship over?

—*Anonymous*

A Well, it will be if the two of you don't stop your passive-aggressive Internet foolishness! So far, you've taken to Facebook, blogspots, e-mail, and advice columns. For the love of snapdragons, why not talk to each other?

Social media are meant to facilitate communication, not create safe distances for flaming. If you care about your friend, call her up. An old-fashioned chat may be just the ticket.

(And for the record: You're right about the wildflowers. If we pick them, how can other people enjoy them?)

# 11

. . . . . . . . . .

# Facebook, Twitter, and
# Other Social Media

*It's Your Party (But You Still Can't Diss Your Sister)*

Facebook is the best thing that's ever happened to my mother-in-law. She's on it constantly, chiming in as soon as my husband or I post a status update: "Who's that?" "What does that mean?" "I've never heard of that band." Recently she sent a message to a friend of mine (whom she'd never met) after seeing a picture of her holding a cigarette in one of my photo albums. Her message: "Smoking is very dangerous. And the color of that sweater doesn't flatter you." I've had it, but my husband thinks I'm overreacting. Am I?

—*Ellie, Santa Barbara, CA*

Ah, parents! Seems like only yesterday they were pecking out unintelligible e-mail messages and pressing Send twenty-four times in a row. And now they're on Facebook, poisoning our relationships one by one.

Call out the National Guard!

Overreacting, Daughter-in-Law? I don't think so. Mumsy's tendency to reach out and touch can have real consequences for you and your husband, at least in terms of retaining friends (and your sanity).

Suggest a simple rule: You and Hubby are fair game. (Sorry, but you are.) Your friends, however, are off-limits—unless they start chatting with her first. It's easy to enforce, requires absolutely no judgment, and will minimize the number of people who open messages from your mother-in-law, asking, "You're wearing THAT?"

Back in the olden days, when I was a sprightly young entertainment lawyer, one of my least promising (pro bono) clients did the unthinkable: He got himself nominated for an Academy Award! Not only that, he invited me to be a part of his posse at the ceremony—at the actual Dorothy Chandler Pavilion in Los Angeles!

Black tie, red carpet! Stars! (Me and stars!)

I hyperventilated for about eight weeks. This was a dream come true.

Now, a smarter person may have realized that "Best Animated Short" is probably not where the action is on Oscar night. What's more, with all the stars in the firmament in attendance, my client (and his lovely parents) and I would probably not be the center of attention. But these thoughts did not occur to me. No, I was far too busy fantasizing about my perfect evening: rubbing elbows with Madonna and Michael Jackson, being seated next to Elizabeth Taylor ("Dinner tomorrow, Liz? I'd love to!"), and attending the after-party at the Chateau Marmont.

Simply put, the *idea* of my Academy Awards evening got the better of me.

Well, you know how this story ends, right?

I wasn't a second-class citizen at the Academy Awards. That would have been a magnificent step up. I wasn't even a fourth-class citizen. I was nothing more than a lowly calf at the film industry's annual cattle drive—and so far from the stage that not even binoculars would have helped me.

And my fantasy was dashed.

# That's Facebook for You Too: An Idea That Seemed Perfect, but Didn't Turn Out That Way

For many of us, social media seemed like a perfect refuge. No more putting up with unreasonable bosses and needy colleagues, no bumping into exes at the gym or relentless in-laws after work. No, Facebook would be the antidote to all that: a dreamy place where we would like everyone we saw, and they'd like us right back. Where the great unwashed would be kept behind the velvet ropes. A place—to borrow a phrase—"where everybody knows your name."

What a party, right?

But then we logged on—and reality bit us in the ass:

Do I have to "friend" my (second) cousin who has done nothing but annoy me all my life? She's already on her third request.

How long do I have to wait before defriending the ex who dumped me via text message? (How about his mother?)

I have a Facebook "friend" and Twitter follower who I barely know in real life. Her status updates and Twitter feeds are MUCH too frequent and, based on what little I know of her, are filled with lies: Yeah, I'm sure she had dinner with Marc Jacobs. Do I tell her how I feel, or just pull the plug?

And just like that, our perfect oasis became just like everyplace else in our lives: riddled with compromise, and forcing us to balance the needs of other people against our own. But still, we cling to the fantasy—and put up with the relentless pokes and cybercupcakes and "Which Disney Princess Am I?" quizzes—all in the hope that this ridiculous, bordering-on-mentally-subnormal place may yet be that perfect idyll we've been after for so long.

Well, it ain't.

And the longer we persist in our fantasy, the more frustrated we become, often displacing our annoyance onto the real-world friends and colleagues we meet online. We behave rudely because our dream has failed to materialize. Well, I hate to be the one to tell you, but that perfect place doesn't exist. And though there may be places "where everybody knows your name," there is virtually no chance that those folk will not, on occasion, work our last nerve. That doesn't entitle us to treat them badly.

So, are you ready for the sad truth? Well, here it is:

Facebook Only *Seemed* Like Someplace Special. But in Fact, It's Just as Annoying as Everyplace Else in the World, and We Have to Treat People There as Well as We Do in Real Life!

Let's look at a few examples. You'll see what I mean.

### To Friend or Not to Friend?

I finally opened a Facebook account. I have seven siblings, two of whom completely annoy me: One is passive-aggressive and the other is always negative. I don't want to spend a minute of my day being "poked" by them or reading their nasty messages. Is it okay to "friend" some of my siblings but not others?

"Now don't be sad," as the musician known as Meat Loaf might have sung, "'Cause five out of seven ain't bad." That's a better than 70 percent sibling-approval ratio—much better than most of us!

But selective friendings among tight-knit groups never work out. Invariably we create hurt and anger, especially in those who are nasty coming out of the gate. And our chances of getting away with "ignoring" friend requests indefinitely—particularly among family and people with whom we're in frequent contact—seem slim. So keep the peace and friend the whole clan.

Remember, though Facebook is relatively new, unpleasant family members and friends have always been free to call and e-mail us, right? But over time, we simply wean them of the habit by slower-than-average response time, and failing to engage them when we do. And before we know it, we've practically eliminated them from our lives. And if it's any consolation, most people lose interest in Facebook after a few months—or seventy thousand man-hours, whichever comes first. Think of it like that new puppy our parents got us when we were seven. We loved the fur off it for the first few weeks, then stuck our mothers with the ugly chores.

Here's another one. This time, involving work friends:

> I've recently received a few Facebook friend requests from people I work with. They're perfectly nice, but they're not *friend* friends; they're just work friends. And I'd like to reserve Facebook for people I really care about. How should I handle this?

Listen, we're free to use Facebook however we want. Some people are there to socialize; others want to network for career advancement or their special causes. A few (apparently) just want to annoy the hell out of us with their numerous hugs and ironic "likes" and endless status updates. So if you want to use the place to meet up with your friends—free of intrusions from the workplace—you're entitled.

But be warned: You're going to hurt some feelings. If these folks weren't fond of you, would they have bothered sending you a friend request? Do you really want to explain your hierarchy of friendship, on which they fall on a low rung? And it's not as if you're going to have intimate discussions on your Facebook page anyway—or at least, you better not!

So, while I'm totally down with your true-friends-only fantasy, what's the point? You're probably already in constant contact with your real friends, and don't need Facebook to help you. And after you've rediscovered a few more high school buddies you'll never really keep up with—and sent a few witty cyber-cupcakes—why bother? Just friend your damn co-workers and call it a day.

Which isn't to say that you should friend every Tom, Dick, and Mary:

> My husband's ex-wife sent me a friend request on Facebook. They've been divorced for ten years and have no contact, but we are friendly with her brother. Can I press the Ignore button? I can't imagine being friends with her.

We can never have too many friends, but we can certainly have too many ex-wives, especially if they're poring over pictures of our family vacation on Cape Cod. Punch the Ignore button and forget about it.

A friendship with an ex-wife's brother is hardly reason to be involved with her, though you do, apparently, have the same taste in men. (And it might be interesting to send her the "Which Beatles Wife Are You: Linda or Yoko?" Facebook quiz.)

And so it goes: Facebook friendships are just an extension of the real-world friendships we've been dealing with since preschool. And as a general matter, it's kinder (and easier) just to say yes.

Or think of it this way: Once you've friended someone, you're one step closer to that ultimate, passive-aggressive hissy fit of our digital age, defriending.

## Giving Friends the Old Heave-Ho!

No question about it, slamming a door shut can be fun. But dramatic gestures start to look pathetic if we overuse them. So defriend sparingly.

I invited a friend to a classical music concert for a Thursday night. She said yes, but later claimed a long business trip, beginning that evening, when I reminded her. The day after the concert, she sent a group e-mail inviting us all to go dancing that night. I said, "I thought you were away on business?" She replied that her trip had been canceled. So I defriended her on Facebook because I believe she lied. Am I overreacting?

Let me put it this way: Yes!

Unless we've got a "smoking gun"—or the kind of telepathic skills that will win us a berth on *America's Got Talent*—it doesn't pay to defriend pals so quickly. In this case, the friend agreed to go to a concert with us, suggesting that she enjoys our company. And even though it didn't work out, she asked us to go dancing with her later in the week. This sounds like a person, who, to para-phrase Sally Field, "likes us—really, really likes us!" So if a friend bails clumsily or just annoys us one afternoon, should we defriend them? Of course not! Friends, whether Gaga-lovers or Grieg heads, do not grow on trees, so preserve them whenever possible.

Take a break if you need one, but don't defriend.

### The Truth Comes Out Even Faster Online!

So how should we deal with online conflicts? Take a look:

> A dear friend proposed visiting me in Seoul, South Korea, where I'm living for a year. Later she sent me an e-mail canceling the trip: "I'm too broke to take a vacation right now." Imagine my hurt when I found pictures of her on Facebook, lying on an (ex-pensive) beach at the same time she was supposed to be visiting me! How can I deal with this without seeming petty?

I've heard of people like this, preferring to frolic on sunny beaches, rather than fighting crowds in noisy cities filled with bad air and traffic jams. Crazy, right?

Here's the thing: We all lie about something—our ages, IQs, how many nights a week we watch dance programs on TV. This particular friend simply calculated that it would be easier on her (and less hurtful to us) if she claimed to cancel the vacation, rather than simply admitting that she'd prefer some sun and fun. The witch!

A few years ago, she probably would have gotten away with it too. Enter Facebook, where the truth pops up like JPEG weeds. But the trouble with confronting friends who reach for the easy lie is that we don't want them doing it again, because that will only hurt us a second time. Go with something like, "I understand that you preferred a beach vacation. Just promise to be honest with me next time, okay?"

That should do it: crisis (and defriending) averted.

Now that you've got your one-two punch—

1. Facebook only seemed like Shangri-la; in fact, it's just like every other place; so
2. Treat your "friends" like you would if you ran into them on the street—try one on your own:

Q A friend of mine is obsessed with Twitter. Her number of daily tweets is out of control. She posts everything she eats (down to the ingredients) and every place she goes (Foursquare!) The worst part is that she acts like she's some sort of celebrity in the Twittersphere. I've stopped following her feed to eliminate my annoyance, but I'd like to be honest with her. Can I tell her that no one cares about her hemp-and-spirulina smoothies?

Now remember, friends don't grow on trees! Also, consider what's really motivating the question. When you've decided how to respond, turn the page and check your response against mine.

Well, it's an epidemic, all right! But this gal's posts about her New Age milk shakes are just a symptom.

Think about it: Our parents paid more attention to us than theirs did to them. It was supposed to make us feel better about ourselves, but only resulted in a flood of "poor me" memoirs instead. And the parents who followed ours pay even closer attention to their brats, which has created a tsunami of Facebook updates and Twitter feeds.

Turns out, Liza Minnelli wasn't the only kid hungry for a stage!

I wouldn't make a fuss about this woman's tweets. It doesn't really sound like the questioner is concerned with her best interests. It seems like he just wants to take her down a peg. And he's already found an easy way to deal with her annoying posts, right? So let's sympathize with her instead, because most of the civilized world seems to share her affliction.

If we've got to weigh in, make it an observation about the culture. Try, "You know, it's hard to miss people when they refuse to go away."

### When the Love Light Dies and Defriending Ensues
#### A How-To Guide

And so it follows, as the night unto the day, that when romance ends, Facebook friendships can become a tad sticky. But judging from the number of letters I've received from men and women who are

FURIOUS at being summarily defriended—or, as they put it, "cut out of my ex's life"—I suggest caution.

One guy simply couldn't bear the sight of all those status updates from his ex or her family members. (*Mary's going to Trader Joe's, Mary feels chipper this morning, Mary's eating Nutella straight from the jar.* Who cares, Mary? It's almost enough to cause the breakup in the first place.) But when this poor fellow defriended his ex, their otherwise amicable breakup turned nuclear. The ex announced to all the world (via her Facebook page) that he'd always been "a lousy lover." She then proceeded to destroy his precious collection of vinyl records. Ouch!

So if you want to be a congenial ex, make no sudden moves, online or otherwise, while nerves are still raw. Leave everything status quo for a few weeks, then begin a meticulous pyramid of defriendings: Prune out the ex's distant relatives, then casual friends, then immediate family and posse—in that order—and leave several days between groups. Boot the ex after a period of pure silence. Start with one month, then add another for every year you were together. Make sure to restart the clock after intervening messages and drunk-dialing episodes! And if amicability isn't your strong suit, wait two and a half minutes after you've retrieved the LAST of your belongings, then defriend your heart out!

My sister-in-law friended me on Facebook. One of my sisters is having a bridal shower this weekend. My sister-in-law's post on Facebook read, "Not looking forward to spending time with the in-laws this weekend." That's right—the in-laws is me! What's the best response to this situation? (Please tell me there can be a response!)

—Ginny B., Montreal

I'd go with "BUSTED!!"—all caps and let the exclamation points fly.

You are in possession of information that could split a peaceable kingdom into Montagues and Capulets. But why unleash it? Your sister-in-law friended you, so she probably wasn't referring to you in her post—just the rest of your lousy family. (And who in their right mind wants to go to a bridal shower?)

Let her know you know, but keep it between the two of you. Screwups like these can bond us if we let them.

# 12

· · · · · · · · ·

## Online Dating

*When True Romance Is Just 10 Million Clicks Away!*

Five minutes before my first in-person meeting with a man I met on Match.com, he called to tell me that he couldn't keep our date: He'd just been hit by a bicycle on the sidewalk and had landed in the emergency room. Something sounded off, so I called the hospital where he said he was, and was told that no such person was there. When I called him back, he insisted that he was.

Several weeks later, I spoke with a woman who had also made a date with this man, several weeks after I did, and he canceled five minutes before their date too, claiming—what else?—that he'd been hit by a bicycle on the sidewalk. When I confronted the guy, he insisted that bike accidents aren't so unusual. How would you handle this?

—*Bonnie, Long Beach, NY*

Well, poetic justice probably requires that you and your pal track down a bicycle built for two and show your online Casanova what the inside of an emergency room really looks like!

But here's an even better idea: Stop communicating with him. This guy is a creep and a liar, probably married and—even worse—using seriously outdated photos of himself in his online profile. Nothing good is going to come from continued engagement with him.

Unfortunately, there's so such thing as a perfect delivery system for eligible men and women. And what the Internet offers in terms of increased volume and speed, it tends to subtract with its profusion of cads and game players. Next time you find one, simply report him to the site's complaint desk and move on to the next guy.

I know it's frustrating when you think you've met the man of your dreams and he turns out to be a serial liar (who can't even come up with fresh material). But rehabilitating online frauds is not your job, and hoping that you'll fix them through protracted interaction will only waste your time and possibly land you in the emergency room yourself—with a case of apoplectic seizures.

Before there was a Carrie Bradshaw—I know, but try to think back that far—before there was HBO, there existed an even crazier quartet of boy-crazed, shopping-obsessed girls.

"Impossible!" you say.

Well, it's true, though the time this foursome spent on TV ran closer to sixty seconds than thirty minutes. (They clocked in at about eleven years of age too, as opposed to the Carrie Clan's grim march toward menopause.) Just bit players—in a television commercial, no less—but they were superstars to me.

*Meet your secret admirer!*

"He's here!" the plain little girl screams, flinging open the front door. "My Mystery Date!"

> *Mystery Date, are you ready for your Mystery Date?*
> *Don't be late! It could be great!*
> *Just open the door for your Mystery Date!*

Then comes the announcer: "It's Mystery Date. The thrilling new Milton Bradley game of romance and mystery that's just for you! And you! And you! And you!"—cutting to each of the hyperventilating girls in turn.

"When you open the door, will your date be a dream—or a dud? Fun and surprises, that's Mystery Date!"

In case you haven't played lately, the game went something like this: Roll the dice, and move your cardboard effigy around the board, acquiring all the glamorous clothes and accessories you could possibly need for one of four thrilling theme dates:

1.  a sporty afternoon on the ski slopes
2.  a fun-filled day at the beach—in a two-piece (!)
3.  a formal dance with a full-length gown
4.  a madcap night of bowling

(I tried not to judge, but bowling—really? And in subsequent editions, Milton Bradley traded the bowling shoes for a picnic lunch. Much better, right?)

Round and round the board you go, and when your piece lands on a corner spot, you may finally throw open the white plastic door at the center of the board to meet your very own Mystery Date: A dreamy dream, whose clothing matched the activity for which you are prepared. You, as in, the winner! Or a different dreamy dream, who was dressed for a different activity—oh, the agony! But there was a third possibility too: That opening the door might reveal the dud—a scruffy mess who no sensible girl would date (though, weirdly, the one who appealed to me most).

You get the point: Land the right stuff and the right guy, and you've got it all, sister!

Well, Internet dating is just like that. You've already got the right stuff. Or you're assembling it as we speak: the bag, the boots, the melted highlights. But who has time to go out and find the right guy or gal? Maybe you work so hard that there's no time for trawling for potential mates. Or maybe you've already burned through the dating pool in your area, or are so finicky that those boys and girls just won't do.

Well, Match.com and eHarmony and Manhunt and Nerve can help. And it couldn't be easier. In fact, it's just like shopping for shoes!

From your cubicle at work or laptop at home (maybe both?), these sites let you click and browse through all your potential mates—and browse and browse some more—until you find the perfect one. Then you exchange three thousand e-mails and text messages until you find something terribly wrong with them, or they find something wrong with you, and then you start all over again.

Sounds like fun, right?

It also leads to some awkward moments that the manufacturer of Mystery Date probably didn't anticipate. Let's take a look—in case you draw one of these wild cards, you'll know just what to do.

### Oh, No! My Mystery Date Is Already Married!

I'm sorry, but it happens—and much more often than you'd think. Maybe these married folks are just passing the time, or looking for some fun on the sly, but the married-but-STILL-looking take up lots of space on the Internet:

I had some bad luck on Match.com: All the guys I met were just cheating on their wives—not that they ever admitted it to me. So I switched to Nerve.com, where I met a terrific guy. And we've been getting along great! Trouble is, when I googled him after our first date, a few online profiles listed him as married. He doesn't wear a wedding ring, and his apartment shows no sign of a wife. (I sense he's divorced.) I'd like him to tell me about his marital status on his own, but I don't want to wait too long. Should I wait? And was googling him okay? My women friends tell me it's normal, but the men tell me I'm crazy.

Sorry about your bum luck, but all those Don Drapers (and other "Mad Men") had to go somewhere, right?

The whole point of the Internet—which we could probably confirm with its inventor, Al Gore—is to check out folks we're interested in dating. (Well, that and free porn.) So google away! Who would this gal's male friends prefer she cyber-search: dudes she's *not* interested in?

But there's a point at which we have to close our laptops and start dealing with the flesh and blood sitting right in front of us. Why not speak with our new (and hopefully divorced) beau?

I'm not sure what people are chatting about on their early dates these days, if not siblings and past relationships? Those were always the one-two punches in my getting-to-know-you arsenal.

If we suspect that our dreamy new boyfriend is already married, there's only one way to find out—and I don't mean logging onto MarriedOrNot.com. Say, "Tell me about the women in your past. Any good skeletons in your closet?" Then return the favor. Trust me, it's useful information. Unless we have Amazing Kreskin–like mind-reading abilities, our "sense" that he's divorced will be cold comfort to us when we discover that his wife and kids have merely decamped to the Hamptons for a spell.

Unmarried? Check.

(Why am I so sure that our mothers and fathers weren't dealing with problems like this?)

Next up:

### Nice to Meet You, but Where's the Mystery Date from the Picture?

At the age of thirty-seven, I find myself unexpectedly single again. So I joined Match.com, where I've chatted with a lot of pretty women, many of whom turn out to be far less pretty (and much older) in real life than their online pictures make them out to be. Is this normal? Is there an etiquette for asking how recent somebody's online pictures are?

Ah, the pleasures of online dating, where half the participants are only killing time while they wait for their 4:00 p.m. conference call, and the serious daters are so finicky that they make 9Lives' Morris the Cat look easygoing by comparison. I'm afraid that some outdated pictures seem to go with the territory too. Everyone wants to look their best, and if that was fifteen years ago, oh well . . .

As a practical matter, focus on profiles with more than one picture: Be on the lookout for radically different hairstyles and clothing styles from different decades. Beware of anyone sporting a Kurt Cobain grunge look. It may seem like yesterday, but that was twenty years ago now. Or the next time you're hitting it off online, try giving to get: "My profile pics were taken at my sister's wedding on Borneo last summer. What about yours?" The response may give you a better sense of the photographic time line.

As for liars and professional retouchers, I'm afraid you're on your own.

Easy, right?

These first two examples point in the "buyer beware" direction of Mystery Dating: It is a big, scary world out there, and we can be hoodwinked pretty easily by mischief-makers. Still, what I know of people makes me suspect that most online daters mean well, even if they have some trouble with execution.

In fact, the most common problem with online dating involves neither trick photography nor stashed wedding rings. It's:

### You Seem Very Nice, Mystery Date, But . . .

I recently joined an online dating site. When I receive a message from a woman I don't find physically attractive, how do I respond? Is no response the best answer? How do I decline politely?

How about building an effigy of the woman and setting it on fire? I'll bet she takes the hint then.

Here's the thing: Online dating can seem like an anonymous business, with all those (typewritten) overtures popping out of the ether. But in fact, the authors of those messages are real, live people—with feelings and everything. So if someone initiates a chat with you online, or sends you a message, respond as politely as you would at a bar or a bus stop.

If this person goes so far as asking you out—even though she has the audacity to not be your cup of tea—how about a simple "No, thanks"? Don't ignore her messages. When we like people, for some sad reason, we can convince ourselves that it's reciprocal, no matter how obvious the truth is to everyone else. They'll just keep bugging you. So be straight with them instead. It may take decades, but these people will get over us eventually—and quite possibly go on to lead semi-productive lives!

### Parting Shot: Be Realistic, Mystery Daters

We all love super-hotties, and wish we could have one of our own. But let's be realistic. Holding out for better may be the American way, but most of us are neither Warren Beatty nor

Faye Dunaway (and it ain't 1967 anymore, Bonnie and Clyde). I'm not asking you to go out with anyone who makes your flesh crawl, but try to keep an open mind. Meeting new people is the whole point of this enterprise, right? No need to play "Princess and the Pea."

And believe it or not, you probably have a physical imperfection of your own. (Even I do!)

In the end, looks fade—they really do. And the qualities that matter—kindness and a sense of humor, not to mention compatibility in TV viewing and tolerance for shared YouTube clips—take a while to sort out. So try to be a little flexible, and don't reject everyone out of hand, okay?

And after you've been flexible, and met the person of your dreams, and actually created something like a relationship, then comes the final question:

### Can't We Shut Down These Annoying Profiles Already?

My boyfriend and I met, several months ago, through an online dating site. I thought everything was going well. But I recently discovered that he's been checking his online dating account regularly. I'm furious! I consider this cheating. Don't you? How should I approach him?

Preferably not with a sharpened meat cleaver in hand!

It's one thing to check your online profile periodically, to see how popular you've been or whether Gisele Bündchen has finally come to her senses and messaged you. It's another to be scaring up dates while your girlfriend is sitting in the next room.

Still, we don't know what kind of agreement these two have about their relationship. (I'm not even going to ask what manner of cybersleuthing our gal used to "discover" that her beau was checking his dating profile.)

A word to the wise: Never assume that you and your honey are on the same page when it comes to something as critical as exclusivity or fidelity. Close your damn laptops and talk it out! And if it never comes up, bring it up: "We seem to be doing really well. You agree? Any interest in closing down our Internet accounts and seeing where this relationship might go?"

It's hard to do. But if you don't ask, you'll never know.

A dear friend fell in love with a cowboy through an Internet dating site. They shared their hopes and dreams, and even discussed marriage and having a baby, although my friend is in her fifties and they'd never met. She planned to move to his state to live with him. When she flew there, they connected for a few days, then he broke up with her. Now she is devastated, and telling her story to anyone who'll listen. She sounds nuts, and I want to protect her. May I tell her to stop?

—Tracey, San Francisco

Hold yer horses, Li'l Lady! Words spoken cannot be unspoken. So unless your friend's sob story includes a heartfelt rendition of "I've Got Spurs That Jingle Jangle Jingle," better to keep quiet and let her vent awhile.

She's grieving and needs your support. This is no time for telling her to swallow her feelings. There will be plenty of time for coolheaded analysis—and vicious mockery—later, when she's feeling better. And while it may seem to us that her romance was more fantasy than reality—an online cowboy, hello?—people make mysterious connections all the time. We can't know what she had with him. And at this point, does it matter?

Your friend may come to regret sharing her troubles with so many people. But it could be worse: At least she's not roping poodles in Golden Gate Park or attacking you for being judgmental. Just take her to the next show of Marlboro Man pictures by Richard Prince. Maybe she'll meet a sensible dentist in a pair of Tony Lama boots.

# PART 5

# Getting Along (with the Folks We're Stuck With)

# Neighbors and Roomies

*How Can We Miss Them When They Won't Go Away?*

We live in a town-house complex where familiarity has bred name-calling, squabbling, and—worse—letters to the IRS over neighbors' questionable tax deductions. My husband and I prefer to keep to ourselves. When one of our neighbors asked to see our newly renovated unit, we declined politely. But she's become quite aggressive about it, and never misses a chance to pester us about seeing our place. What should we do?

—Liza, Boca Raton

Ding-dong! Suspiciously old Girl Scout at the door selling Thin Mints.

It's your house, Liza, so you can do what you like—including installing two beefy bouncers at the front door with a red velvet rope. But why bother? Do you really want to keep reenacting *High Noon* in front of the palmetto bushes and *The Fugitive* in the carport?

If it's just the principle, cave. Let the rude old bird snoop to her heart's content and put this matter behind you. Your pesky neighbor shows no sign of taking your hints, and this hardly seems worth starting another feud in your decidedly unpeaceable kingdom.

On the other hand, if you and your husband have installed an illegal indoor lap pool, stick with your moral high ground.

You know that expression "Life is not a dress rehearsal"?
You get it: There are no second chances to live life. No take 2s

or do-overs. So get out there and, in the words of a famous sneaker, "Just do it."

Fine. Life is not a dress rehearsal.

But do you know what *is* a dress rehearsal? Our relationships with our neighbors and roommates, that's what.

Think about it. They're always around, just like the more important folks in our lives—lovers and kin. And because they're there, they tend to witness our most delicate moments (and we, theirs): the disheveled walks of shame on Sunday morning, the furious spouses screaming epithets from the carport, all those pubescent children slamming bedroom doors.

We share a zone of intimacy with these people: Not close (necessarily), but close by. And even though we don't care about them nearly as much as we care about our loved ones, we still try to behave well with them.

Why?

Because we know we're going to see them again—and again and again and again. And we want to avoid the awkwardness of knowing we behaved badly when we do—hiding out in the garage for weeks after our hissy fit, or feeling our stomachs clench into knots at the mere sight of them.

So here's an idea: Let's put these neighbors and roommates to good use. Think of them as crash test dummies for the more important relationships in our lives. We'll practice on them!

Learning how to extricate ourselves from our neighbors' endless weekend barbecues (or roommates' tofu suppers) is a superb dry run for getting out of our brother-in-law's FOURTH baptism party for his firstborn. And responding calmly to our neighbors' barbs, whether called- or uncalled-for, is excellent practice for dealing with our boyfriends' (or girlfriends') snark.

What's even better, if we screw it up with our neighbors and roommates, it'll be a shame, for sure—but nothing like screwing it up with our wives or mothers, where the consequences can be serious. There's no alimony for Neighbors Nancy or Ned. And no lifetime of awkward Thanksgivings with them either. If things get really hairy, maybe they'll move.

Turns out, neighbors and roommates are: Relationship Lite!

It's win-win: excellent practice for the skills required in our more important relationships, but relatively consequence-free if we blunder.

First up, the golden rule for dealing with roommates and neighbors:

### Whenever Possible, Let It Slide

As anyone with occasionally annoying loved ones knows—am I leaving anyone out?—picking our battles is critical. Otherwise, we'd end up fighting 24-7, which may be great for Civil War reen-actors, but most of us have lives to lead (and reality TV to watch). Well, it's the same with pesky neighbors: Whenever possible, let a smile be your bazooka. Those garbage pails sitting at the end of their driveway for too long? No problem! Gladys Kravitz hawk-eyeing you from her kitchen window? Just smile and move along!

For instance:

> We live next door to the county jail, so our neighbors are a bunch
> of convicted criminals. What's the right thing to do when passing
> two sheriff's deputies and a guy in handcuffs who's chained to leg
> irons? Ignore them? Turn away?

When I sang for the inmates at Folsom Prison—no, hang on,
that was Johnny Cash, wasn't it?

I smile and nod every time I see a neighbor, whether it's the
lovely one from across the hall, or the meanie from downstairs
(who I know, for a fact, doesn't recycle). And though I've never
crossed paths with a man in shackles, I'd like to think I have the
panache to pull off a blasé nod. I hope you do too. That jailbird
may have broken the law, but he's still a person, after all. (No
sense in giving offense: That con is probably going to be paroled
one day, right?)

Think of it like this: Smiling at criminals is excellent practice for smiling at your mother-in-law after she emerges from your
apartment's only bathroom after hogging it for forty-five minutes
when she knows you have a job interview to prepare for.

What good is fighting going to do you? Just let it slide.

Here's another:

> My boyfriend and I had our neighbors over for dinner. We made
> a fabulous meal, and used our best china and exquisite Georg

Jensen silver. The next day, we noticed that a silver teaspoon was missing. We looked high and low for it, to no avail. I have a feeling that one of the neighbors stole it. I'd like to send them thank-you-for-coming cards and add, "A teaspoon is missing, and we miss it." My boyfriend thinks I'm crazy, but I want that spoon back. May I?

This reminds me of that old expression: Some friends are silver, and others—well, just steal it.

I'm with the boyfriend on this one. Don't send notes about missing teaspoons, or hang "Wanted" posters of your neighbors in the post office. Things get lost, and sometimes they turn up again. Thievery, on the other hand, is much rarer. If the spoon fell into one of our neighbors' bags by accident, they'll let us know. And if they stole it, what on earth would a note accomplish? Last I heard, thieves aren't big on returning their loot. Better to search eBay instead: It's loaded with Jensen spoons.

And as hard as it may be to keep our lips zipped, just imagine trying to rebound with these folks, when we run into them at the market, *after* we've accused them of stealing our cutlery.

Just let it go. It'll be great practice for when your boyfriend asks if his jeans make his ass look big—and they do.

Okay, here's one more—for when the going gets really tough:

One of my neighbors signed my petition against a third neighbor, but it turns out, she only did it to gather information for the offending neighbor. She piles her plastic pots and other garbage against her house, in my direct sight line. And she falsely accused me of flooding her basement. How to handle such a neighbor?

Enough! I don't even live in this neighborhood, and I've got a stomachache. I'm also skeptical of sagas where one party is all Glinda the Good Witch and the other, Boom Boom the Bad. Life rarely unfolds that way.

Another term for "letting things slide"—a militaristic one, no less—is "détente," which I heartily endorse in cases like this. So if your neighborly relations spiral out of control, take a deep breath, think of your loved ones and good health, and put the conflict out of your head—for at least a year. Unplug!

Disengagement makes sense here because engagement isn't making things better, and is possibly making them worse. So consider plantings for the windows that face the (presumably legal) lawn garbage—and maybe a move in the near future.

But isn't there a middle ground between ignoring small problems and retreating (in a cold fury) to separate corners? Of course there is. Letting things slide isn't our only option when it comes to roommates and neighbors.

It's simply our first line of defense.

Many times, we can feel free to share our concerns with neighbors and roommates. But remember: While these folks may feel like strangers, they're not. We're going to see them the day after the confrontation too. So take it slow and easy.

## If You Need to "Speak" with a Neighbor, Do It Gently

The guy I share my apartment with is a total stoner. The fumes leach from his bedroom across the hall into mine. I have nothing against pot, but the constant smell is making me sick. Otherwise, he's a great roommate. Should I call our landlord? Or the police?

What, in the name of Cagney and Lacey, do you expect the fuzz to do—other than prompt your (mostly) excellent roommate to move out?

Before calling the authorities on roommates and neighbors—or hiring the Sopranos, for that matter—and long before tying ourselves into furious tight little knots, try airing our concerns (har har!) with the folks in question. Who knows? They may be sympathetic to our troubles, given half a chance.

If the roommate's a toker, ask him to open his window and tape the gap beneath his bedroom door. Farewell, foul fumes! (Not that I'd know firsthand.) And if that fails, try bribing him with a boxed set of *Harold & Kumar* DVDs. It's much easier than finding a new roommate, no? The same goes for barking beagles and Katy Perry played at high volumes on auto-repeat: A calm word, delivered at the right moment, does wonders.

More on that:

I've had the same elderly neighbors for years. But recently their geriatric sexcapades have gone out of control. Unfortunately, we share a bedroom wall. Their daily fun begins at 5:00 a.m., about the time I wake up to pray. I bang on our shared wall in hopes of shaming them, to no avail. Otherwise, they're very nice and old enough to be my grandparents. What more can I do?

News flash: Old people are people too—with sexual urges and everything. So how about praying for greater tolerance while you're at it? (Though that probably won't diminish the banging of the old folks' bed against your shared wall.)

For that, a polite note should do the trick. No need for pounding on walls (or floors or ceilings). Try, "There's quite a racket coming from the bedroom in the morning. Please move your bed. Many thanks—and rock on!"

No need to suffer. Just wait until after your exasperation has passed and address the problem calmly—the same way we'll (hopefully) handle our girlfriend's annoying habit of taking food from our plate, or our boyfriend's propensity for interrupting our best stories: not by snapping, in the moment, but with a quiet word, delivered later on.

The same "think first" principle holds when the problem isn't a nuisance, but a judgment call. Don't rush into anything:

I just moved into a tiny apartment in Brooklyn with two roommates: a man and a woman. We get along swimmingly. Recently I've developed a crush on the guy. We seem to have loads to talk about. We went to the movies last week, and though nothing happened between us, I find myself even more interested in him. May I ask him out on a date, without breaking every rule in the roommate bible?

Obviously, this gal is new in town, because she's not thinking like a New Yorker yet: Romantic connections may come and go, but teeny-tiny apartments are forever!

In cases like these, our best bet for preserving a happy household (or neighborhood) is to express our feelings, while respecting theirs. Tell the roommate that you like spending time with him, and wonder if he'd be interested in dinner sometime? No need to jump the gun: Keep your post-dinner plans for a steamy make-out session to yourself.

If he begs off, case closed. And even if he agrees, watch out for platonic signals: like calling other women hot in front of you, or belching like a trucker. (But wear your sexy lingerie, just in case!) And since these are early days, avoid confiding in your other roommate about the crush, but don't lie if she asks—unless she's involved with the guy, in which case you may want to stretch the truth for as long as possible.

See? With a little extra sensitivity, we can express ourselves and preserve the possibility of bumping into each other in the communal kitchen, the next morning, without extreme awkwardness or beet-red blushing.

Unfortunately, that won't always be possible. Human beings being what we are, sometimes an explosion will occur. That's life! And when they do, the recovery is all.

### After the Explosion, or the Do-Over

To thank me for going out of my way for them, again and again, my next-door neighbors invited me to Sunday brunch at a nice restaurant. While we were dining, the waiter placed two dozen oysters on the table. My hosts told me they were just for the hostess—and that I couldn't have any. I was dumbfounded. So I excused myself to the bathroom and marched right out of the restaurant. Later I sent them a message saying that I didn't appreciate being treated like a second-class citizen and had no interest in seeing them ever again. The hostess replied that the invitation was for the "base brunch" only, not for extras. Was I wrong?

Not to worry! There were so many helpings of wrong at that brunch table, everyone can have seconds. For starters, who polishes off twenty-four oysters all by herself . . . on top of eggs Benedict and mimosas? Seems like plenty to go around. But while the hosts' "paws off my Prince Edwards" policy was rude, it was hardly reason to storm out of the restaurant like Alexis Carrington from *Dynasty.*

Next course, correspondence: Your message was a tad operatic. Never seeing people again over . . . oysters? And the hosts' reply was just as strange, as if brunch invitations came with fine print, like on the back of "get one free" coupons.

So much bad behavior—not to mention your next-door status—almost begs for a do-over, though not at a restaurant, I beg of you. Make it a starting-over drink at one of your houses, where *everyone* is offered a glass of champagne. No rehashing of the brunch debacle either. Just patch it over and move forward.

Knowing how to rebound from fights is a valuable tool. No need to let a storm cloud hover for years—or escalate into Hurricane Louise. Just stop the madness, take a breath, then reapproach with an easy smile. What's more, it's excellent practice for when we explode at our mothers for criticizing our boyfriends, or vice versa. (And for the record, she does NOT look like a Marx Brother!)

Here's another:

> Our state is considering a constitutional amendment that would prevent gay people from marrying. Our neighbors have two signs on their lawn supporting the measure—two!—as well as decals on their ugly minivans. My boyfriend and I are gay and have lived next door to these people for years. I respect differences of opinion, but this seems personal. So one night, I pulled up those lawn signs and hid them in my garage. Now what should I do?

I wish I could say "cart them to your local dump." With so many of our neighbors jobless and losing their homes, and with international crises looming around every corner, this seems like a strange moment to keep people who want to marry from marrying. (Trust me, there's enough confetti to go around.)

But we may not destroy our neighbors' signs. Nor may we set their garbage pails on fire or trample their flower beds. What we may do—but only if we promise to remain calm while doing so—is walk next door, explain how personal the issue is to us, apologize for taking their signs, and ask them to reconsider their position. (Yes, we should return the signs too.) Who knows what will come of that conversation? They may still support the ban on gay marriage, but at least they will have heard a persuasive case from the thoughtful sign thief next door.

We may not always be able to stop our bad behavior, in advance, but we can try to minimize its impact, going forward, while doing our utmost to make our neighborhood one that Mister Rogers would be proud-ish to call his own.

### When the Problem Is—Us!

It was bound to happen. Our neighbor has lodged a complaint against—who, me? Why, that son of a . . . Now don't get all defensive. Or apologize right away either. When neighbors or roommates have a gripe, just listen to the problem first.

In fact, commit to not committing yourself right away:

> I was washing my car outside my house when an elderly woman, out walking her dog, kindly informed me that people in our neighborhood don't wash their cars in front of their homes. Then she whispered, "It's low class." But she made it sound so sweet and polite that I didn't know how to respond. Am I violating the social graces?

It's a strange arbiter of social graces who objects to a neighbor cleaning his car on the street, while she parades her poodle on a mission of public defecation, no? Our neighbors are entitled to express their opinions, and I applaud that the elderly neighbor, in this case, did so politely. We should hear them out, and be careful not to respond too quickly or get carried away by annoyance or the embarrassment of the moment.

If you're not absolutely sure about how to respond, just say, "Let me think about it and get back to you."

In this case, I wouldn't give the complaint much more than a second's thought. It would be one thing if our neighbor were objecting to water waste in a time of drought. She would have given you something to think about then. But since her argument seems to be that you're turning the neighborhood into an episode of *The Beverly Hillbillies*, I'd carry on with washing the car. (Though you may want to stop hunting possum in the front yard.)

But sometimes our neighbors will have a point that may not be immediately clear to us. That's where the listening, first, comes in handy:

My next-door neighbor in my apartment building must either hate music or go to bed at 8:00 p.m. She knocked on my front door last week to ask me to turn down the bass. Then yesterday, she slipped a note under my door. I want to be nice, so I wrote "Sorry" on her note and slipped it back to her. But I'm growing fed up with her complaints. Isn't it outrageous for her to request lower volume in the early evening?

Uh, no! I hate to break it to you, Janis Joplin, but your neighbor isn't necessarily a music hater or settling in for an evening of *Golden Girls* reruns. She may simply not like your taste in music, or prefer to rock out when *she* chooses. What if the shoe were on the other foot and our neighbor loved Clay Aiken?

Here's the thing: If our neighbors can hear our music at their place, then it's too loud. So if a pounding bass line is important to you—and I can certainly understand why it might be—either speak with your neighbor about her daily schedule, or invest in a set of headphones so you can enjoy your music whenever, and however, you like.

So, no rushes to judgment, defensive or otherwise. Just hear them out and think it over. Consult your friends if necessary—or write to me! Remember: It's the odd problem for which we can't find a reasonable compromise.

Okay, last one:

My neighbor walks up to my window and talks to my cat. She doesn't acknowledge my husband or me. She just stands there, speaking into our home. We took the cat in last year as a stray. We posted signs around the neighborhood, and learned that neighbors had been feeding her but weren't able to give her a home. So we did, and had her spayed and vaccinated. Since then, this neighbor often says I "took the cat" she was feeding. I feel uncomfortable with her peering in. Any ideas?

—*Julie, Stockbridge, MA*

Note to Robert Frost: It's not just fences. Good drapes and venetian blinds make good neighbors too.

It sounds as if you acted just right, Julie—at least from Kitty's perspective. And your neighbor sounds a little passive-aggressive. So why not help her out? Say, "I'm sensing some tension over the cat. I hope you agree that she's better off living with us than out of doors. You're welcome to come see her too. Just give a knock, and we'll answer. But can we leave the peeping to pervy teenage boys?"

A restraining order probably does the trick too.

Meow.

# 14

· · · · · · · · ·

## Kids and Parenting

*When There Aren't Enough Time-Outs in a Day*

Q My family hosted some friends and their children for dinner. After dessert, their tween daughter returned her spoon to the table, leaned forward, and began licking her plate. I waited, dumbfounded, for her parents to correct her, but they never said a thing! I didn't want to embarrass the girl or her parents, so I didn't say anything either. But my younger kids were fascinated by her behavior. What should I have done?

—Heather, Newport News, VA

A You mean, other than passing her your pots and pans to lick clean?

My hunch is that the tweeny bopper was trying to provoke her parents into a wild rumpus. Mercifully, they didn't take the bait—in front of you anyway. You did the right thing too, Mummy, by keeping mum. Never discipline other people's kids when they're there to do it themselves! Just follow up with your own kids later, and make sure they understand how silly Pamela the Plate Licker's behavior was.

Sometimes we can't see what's right in front of us.

Take a look at the black-and-white picture above. So what do you see? Two people facing each other in profile, or a Grecian urn? Well, they're both there.

It's the same with music. Nearly everyone's got a cute story about a song lyric they consistently misheard, reworking it into a daffy lyric of their own. "I'll never leave your pizza burnin'," for instance, in place of the Rolling Stones' sexy rock anthem "I'll never be your beast of burden." Or "The ants are a-blowin' in the wind," instead of Bob Dylan's "answer."

And this same thing happens, metaphorically speaking, all the time. Is there a better way to describe the machinery of a Reese Witherspoon or Sandra Bullock romantic comedy? For the first ninety minutes, the gals are simply blind to the love interest that's been under their noses since the first reel. The truth was right there, but they missed it—or mangled it a little.

But all these examples pale compared with the selective blindness (and deafness) of parents when it comes to their kids' occasionally lousy behavior. Practically no human interactions involve quite as much willful un-seeing and heel-digging-in as those involving children, whether ours or someone else's. Friends and neighbors can't seem to hold themselves back from weighing in on the tykes' bad behavior. And parents can be counted on to insist that these eyewitnesses are dead wrong, even when presented with compelling evidence to the contrary.

It makes a kind of sense. We love our kids so much, and see such wonderful qualities in them. To us, they're often the walking, talking manifestations of our best and most vulnerable selves. No criticism required! And if there were a legitimate problem with our little spawn, surely we'd see it ourselves, right? Not necessarily.

Consider the following:

Some good (and usually reasonable) friends brought their two sons, ages nine and twelve, to our place one evening. After dinner, the adults played cards, and the children went off to play. At one point, I found the boys jumping on the family-room sofa and asked them to stop, which they did. After they left, I discovered that the boys had caused some major damage, so I called our friends to let them know. Far from apologizing, the parents claimed that I'm responsible, since we weren't all in the same room. They also accused me of failing to supervise the boys and said that I should have brought the jumping to their attention immediately. What do you make of this?

Let's hear it for (occasionally unreasonable) friends and dinner guests!

Because if abdicating parental responsibility were as simple as temporarily changing address, America would be more mobile than it already is. Your friends' kids are *their responsibility*, no matter which room of your house they're in.

Most parents I know would have checked on their children a couple of times during the course of the evening—and those kids are middle-aged. And while you might have mentioned the trampoline act to the parents, I can understand why you didn't: You thought you'd handled it. My hunch is that your pals heard the story as an attack on their darling boys, so they dug themselves into a defensive, NRA-style position ("Kids don't break sofas;

derelict hosts who don't supervise them do") rather than simply apologizing for the damage.

Why would reasonable people do this?

Who knows? Maybe they can't bear to think of their sons as sofa-stompers. Or maybe (as I suspect), we turn our kids into little ego extensions of ourselves, and just can't bear the criticism.

### Where Children Are Concerned, Parents Often Dig In Hard and Fast

So either let your sofa go or prepare for full-scale war. Of course, menschier folk would simply have offered to pay for the damage, but when it comes to other people's kids—even sensible people's kids—all bets are off. In fact, you're lucky the boys didn't burn your house down. The parents might have blamed you for living too far from the fire station.

Lesson No. 1 for Parents:

If your kid breaks it, just apologize

and whip out the old checkbook.

Corollary for Non-Parents:

If the parent blames you instead,

don't be surprised.

So what's the solution? Excluding kids from your parties?
Hardly:

We're giving a big party. In our invitation we made it clear, in
a polite way, that this would be an adults-only affair. But some
guests have insisted on bringing their children and are deeply offended that we're not giving in. Our home is not child-friendly,
and some kids are impossible. We decided it would be worse to
make exceptions, so we've gone with a blanket rule: Get a sitter
or send regrets. Are we wrong?

Blood is thicker than water, which may explain my continued
conviction that my brother is not a moron—as well as your pals'
determination to drag their kids to your adult party. But note:
Blood is also harder to get out of the living-room rug. So you did
nothing wrong, dear hosts.

The kindest gloss here may be that parents love their kids
so much that they assume everyone else does too. They might
even agree that a general rule prohibiting kids from your fancy
parties is your prerogative—as long as you make an exception
for their little terrors. Still, your friends go too far when they
badger the people lavishing them with food and drink about the
guest list.

A party for adults is perfectly reasonable. When I was a kid,
adults rarely invited us to their shindigs. It helped us understand
that we were not the center of the universe. Today's tykes may

well have a harder time with this concept, since many of their parents arrange their adult lives around the hobbies and sporting events of those not yet able to read, drive a car, or vote (except on *American Idol*).

So if you want to give a party for the mature set, go for it.

And parents: I don't mean to sound grinchy, but if you can't find child care, stay home! An afternoon in the park with a nine-year-old is terrific, but a cocktail party hijacked by the Wii, or whiny requests for chicken fingers, gets old fast.

Lesson No. 2 for Parents:
The rest of us probably aren't as enthralled
with your kids as you are.
Corollary for Non-Parents:
Somehow, parents never believe this.

Not even the just-for-kiddies playdate is exempt from trouble:

My best friend and I have crawling babies who put everything they find in their mouths. So my husband and I don't allow shoes in our home. Unfortunately, this same friend has a habit of picking dead skin from her lip and scratching her scalp, then flicking what she collects under her nails onto the floor. I don't want my son ingesting this—or her daughter either, for that matter! I've asked her if she needs a tissue, but she misses my point. Do I need to phase her out of my life?

Wild guess: First kid?

New parents have two choices: Pour yourself a big glass of chardonnay and relax—like our parents and their parents before them—or drive yourself as nutty as Catherine Deneuve in *Repulsion* as you fixate on the increasingly grotesque things your little angel might shove into his piehole.

Because scalp slough is just the beginning! As parents, we're charged with keeping our children safe. But the world is overflowing with gunk, and we can't control our kids' every waking moment any more than we control our partners. (Not that the world wouldn't be a better place if we could!) So let the head-scratcher scratch and put her shoes back on. Focus on immunizing your baby and feeding him well. Read to him every chance you get. But he's going to swallow a few nickels any way you play it. So you might as well relax—and stock up on some latex gloves.

Lesson No. 3 for Parents:

Try to relax. Your kids aren't made of glass.

Corollary for Non-Parents:

Try not to be offended by your friends' belief
that your sole purpose in life is to infect their
precious children. They don't mean it. Really.

These lessons and corollaries can serve us in all sorts of child-
related pickles, even as the children in question grow older. Try
choosing the right one to solve the following Social Q's:

My niece and nephew, now ages sixteen and eighteen, have
never once thanked me for the annual birthday and holiday
gifts I send. It hurts my feelings. Last year, I even sent a tactful
e-mail on the subject to both of them. Neither replied! Do I
keep buying gifts? Or should I tell on them to their mother (my
sister)?

No one likes a tattletale, Auntie. And rubbing your sister's
nose in the ingratitude of her nearly adult children will probably
backfire on you. This is consistent with the First Corollary: Don't
be surprised if parents blame you for their kids' lousy behavior.
What's more, you've already made your (completely reasonable)

point directly to the gift recipients, and their ignoring your e-mail speaks volumes.

So vote with your pocketbook and save the booty for people with the good sense to thank the goose who lays consistently golden eggs.

Move on!

As will we:

I've been asked by good friends to be the godfather to their new-born son. I'm an atheist and would be one of THREE godfathers to this child. I don't feel comfortable with the commitment to raise the kid if something should happen to his parents. May I refuse this request without giving offense?

Beware! This is a classic example of Lesson No. 2: Friends of new parents must either act as if the newborn were the most ex-traordinary thing since Haley Joel Osment in *The Sixth Sense* or suffer the consequences. Oftentimes, parents just don't get that we're not as into their kids as they are.

Fortunately, religious feeling is not required for the task at hand—but gifts are! No need to worry about raising the child ei-ther. Your friends only want to include you in the happy occasion. They wouldn't entrust you with their precious bundle if you were Dr. Oz. And I don't believe you can refuse this gig without giv-ing offense—unless, perhaps, in a fit of self-denigration, you hurl yourself to the floor and cry out that you're not worthy. They'll agree in a hot second!

Okay, last one:

> My thirteen-year-old son has just started going out with girls. I think he comes on a little strong: first calling, then texting, then calling again to see if she's gotten the text. I suspect the girls find all this communication annoying, and I'd like to tell him to take it slower. But my wife thinks we should stay out of it. How about you?

Classic Lesson No. 3: Relax, Dad! Sonny is not made of glass.

Part of me thinks you should speak with your son about phone etiquette—the same way you taught him to shake hands when he was introduced. But the thirteen-year-old in me keeps rising up to say, This is not about the phone; it's about your son's burgeoning romantic life. So I'd stay out of this, unless you really liked *Portnoy's Complaint*.

Nothing you say will overcome your son's strong impulse to reach out (again and again) to the object of his affection—until his pride grows as wounded as his ardor is bold, which will probably take several years, several girls, and a calming of the hormonal waters. Interference by you will only make you a handy target for his rage.

But if you simply must weigh in, incorporate a story about your own excessive behavior in the throes of adolescence. It might be good for bonding. (And a pith helmet couldn't hurt.)

**War of Wills: When Parenting Styles Collide**

No two snowflakes are exactly alike, and neither are any two parents. Even less like them are non-parents who wish to dip occasionally into the waters of parenting.

My advice: Don't!

Just take care of your own kids, and let them take care of theirs. Trust me: No one wants your two cents.

*My friend likes his young kids to call all adults by their surname (Mr. or Ms. Smith). But I prefer they call me Michael.*

Who cares what you prefer? When you have kids, let them call you whatever you like, but your friend has made a decision about how he'd like his children to speak with adults. So defer to him.

We were at a resort-town movie theater that was small and dirty, with sticky floors. A family of four came in with a large box of popcorn and sat in front of us. The parents and one child went out again. The remaining child, a girl of about seven, accidentally spilled the popcorn all over the floor. She looked around furtively, then picked up the popcorn and put it back in the box. When her family returned, she said nothing about the accident, and they all began to eat. Should we have said something?

—*Bob, Ithaca*

*My neighbor's twelve-year-old daughter dresses like a hooker when she goes to school. (In fact, you'd describe her skirts, not in inches above her knees but in millimeters beneath her privates.) I think it's disgraceful.*

So dress your own kid differently! But keep your views about the neighbor girl to yourself. That's right: defer. Because unless you're this kid's homeroom teacher or personal shopper, both of whom have a right to weigh in on the matter of the little lass's wardrobe, stay out of it.

It's hard enough to raise a kid without every Tom, Dick, and Harry weighing in. And in my experience, the Toms, Dicks, and Harrys with the most to say about other people's kids tend to be the people that parents want to hear from least. So button it up, okay?

Well, Bob, that depends on how you feel about letting your fellow man eat popcorn laced with dried-up soda and everything else that's been tracked in on the bottoms of shoes—honest country dirt, motor oil, and even a dollop of dog poo.

My first impulse was to advise you to keep quiet and let the little girl enjoy her vacation. The risks are probably no greater than taking a dinner mint from a communal bowl at a restaurant. And I hated to embarrass the girl. But then I began to worry: What if the previous occupant of her seat had fertilized his lawn with toxic pesticide—or was a professional dog walker?

So let's warn the family without humiliating the child. In fact, let's compliment her. "Your daughter is so thoughtful," you might say to the parents. "She accidentally spilled her popcorn on the floor, and picked up every kernel." The girl is a star, and no one eats the filthy popcorn

Note to the parents of first graders: This is probably happening to you as we speak.

# If It's Not One Thing,
# It's Your Mother

*Finessing Family Friction*

Every Sunday, my mother-in-law hosts a big family lunch: all her kids and their spouses and grandkids. I actually enjoy going with my wife and baby daughter. But lately, my father has started manipulating invitations—by whining that he's lonely since his (third) wife threw him out. I love my father, but he's very self-centered and dominates the conversation at these lunches with endless stories about himself. I'd like to stop him from attending, so that my wife's family can enjoy themselves. How can I tactfully make that happen?

—*Marcus, Chicago*

Our families don't just push our buttons, Marky Mark, they invented them. So, while you're cringing up a storm at these lunch parties—dying inside at every one of your father's endless yarns—your in-laws probably barely notice Dear Old Dad. They simply don't care about him half as much as you.

Rather than excluding him from the party—which might end up like *Stella Dallas*, with Barbara Stanwyck gazing through her in-laws' window in the rain—why not speak with the Old Man? Try, "Can you do me a favor, Dad? Susie's family isn't as gregarious as you. Let's ask lots of questions to draw them out."

It will never work, but it's worth a shot, and probably beats making your father eat lunch by himself.

We only get one family. (Thank the Baby Jesus!)

When they're gone, we can't replace them. So it's worth going the extra mile to keep them in our lives. You never know when you might need a bone-marrow transplant. And kvetching aside, family relationships are powerful and unique. Neither our oldest pals nor our best mates have been there (for us) in quite the same way as our families, both as firsthand witnesses and collaborators in the formative events of our lives, watching us and shaping us as we came into being. They were there when we discovered we had a knack for music—and also when we insisted on wearing Frye boots with short pants to the first day of third grade.

That's also why these relationships can be so explosive, often marred by hissy fits and feuds, not to mention prolonged periods of angry silence. No one can piss us off quite as efficiently as our kin. And try as we might, it's nearly impossible to turn the volume down.

But not to worry. I have a plan:

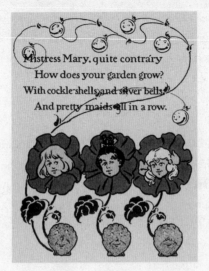

Mistress Mary, quite contrary
How does your garden grow?
With cockle shells and silver bells,
And pretty maids all in a row.

### The "Mary, Mary, Quite Contrary" Program for
### Finessing Friction with the Family

The program is not complicated. But that doesn't mean it will be easy to pull off. In essence, let's do the 180-degree opposite of what our instincts tell us to do with our families. When we want to zig, zag instead.

Trust me, it's extremely effective.

### Your Counterintuitive Guidelines for
### Dealing with Rough Relations:

1. When squabbles break out, keep quiet.
2. When icy silence descends, speak up (gently).

3. When relatives try to draw you into their family feuds,
   resist—no matter how tempted you are to pile on.
4. Never get between your mate and their relations. (Hopefully,
   they'll do the same for you.)

Take a look:

My daughter, who is forty-four and divorced, is stuck in a time
warp: She dresses in Woodstock tie-dye, has her hair styled as if it
were 1950, and wears no makeup at all. On the other hand, she's
slim, has a prestigious job, and owns her own home. She would
love to find love again, but gets extremely upset when I suggest
upgrades in her appearance. How do I get her to "gild the lily"
without alienating her?

You mean, after forty-four years, it still comes down to "You're
wearing *that?*" Mommy already knows that her daughter responds
angrily to her beauty tips—and still she weighs in. Do any of you
mothers (or daughters) out there think the dynamic is going to
change at this stage? (Me neither.)

Remember Rule No. 1: If it's going to start a fight, keep quiet!
(And if you're not sure, assume it will.)

That doesn't mean we can't enlist neutral parties to help us.
How about a gift certificate to a good salon for Hippie Chick's
forty-fifth birthday? Or maybe to a nice boutique that's loaded with
personal shoppers and carries a minimal number of fringed vests
and boots? And while Daughter is thus engaged, Mommy Dearest

can break into her house and steal the nasty tie-dye, which she can donate to the Grateful Dead's Eightieth Birthday Tour.

Win-win!

Next up, the Sounds of Silence:

> For my genealogy research, I asked my sister about her former and current husbands. She told me she didn't want her abusive ex to appear on our family tree. I said that would be lying because they were, in fact, married. She became hysterical and wept, so I let the matter drop. We haven't spoken in weeks, and I still feel wrong about omitting factual information from our genealogy. What should I do?

Fortunately, preparers of family trees—unlike say, witnesses in federal court—are not sworn to tell the (whole) truth. And if a sister is so traumatized by her abusive ex that the mere thought of him in our genealogical records reduces her to tears, leave him out! Doesn't her peace of mind take priority over a chart? (Then again, I'm no genealogist, nor do I know how prone this sister is to crying jags.)

But more importantly, remember Rule No. 2: Do not let chilly silences linger! Speak up: "Gosh, I'm sorry I upset you! You're more important to me than a stupid family tree."

If it makes you feel better, take a cue from baseball fans contemplating the batting records of steroid-injecting sluggers: Just insert a teeny-tiny asterisk on the genealogy that only you can see.

So far, our family frictions have been one-on-one affairs. But often (nearly always, in fact) family members will attempt to triangulate their troubles with other relatives and draw us in.

What then?

Resist!

Take your cue from the great Revolutionary War hero, Nathan Hale. Even as the nasty Brits were slipping a noose around his slender neck, Nathan would not divulge this country's secrets: "I only regret that I have but one life to lose for my" . . . er, family.

Take a look:

For personal reasons, I haven't spoken with my brother in three years. My son keeps in touch with him regularly. I recently received a diagnosis of lung cancer and had part of my lung removed. I've been hospitalized a number of times. And I lost my beloved Yorkshire terrier. But when my brother asked my son how I was, I heard him answer, "Well, thanks." Would I be wrong to tell my son to be honest with my brother about my problems?

Terrible as we might feel about this woman's run of bad luck, it doesn't change the answer: There's a wee difference between honoring thy mother and entering into her blood feuds.

Mommy's raised a wise child to stay out of hers.

It's a classic example of Rule No. 3: Steer clear of your relatives' squabbles! Getting involved is not going to help, and will probably only alienate one of the combatants. Let them resolve their beefs themselves.

But there's a side dish of Rule No. 2 here, as well: Never let silences fester, even (and especially) if we're in the right. It sounds as if our sickly sister wants to be in touch with her brother again; she just doesn't want to make the first move. By getting her son to share her woes, she's hoping her brother blinks—and makes the call. But shouldn't all the serious challenges she's faced put the silly standoff with her brother into better perspective?

Pick up the phone and dial! Our brothers will probably be thrilled to hear from us, and we'll be glad we did it too.

And if it's a big disaster, blame me!

Last one—on the importance of staying neutral where our spouse's (and dear friends') family members are concerned:

> My husband's brother is married to a woman who participates in many charities. We're invited to buy tickets to all her summer fund-raisers. For most of the year, this sister-in-law and her husband are civil, but distant—except when she wants us to support one of her causes. My husband thinks we owe her a personal response every time, as in, "Dear S-I-L, We're sorry, but..." I think he's insane! The response card goes back to the charity, not to her, and she probably invites hundreds of her "closest" friends. What do you think?

Feel the love?

It seems not to have occurred to our letter writer that her husband may be troubled by the chilly relations with his brother and that he's compensating with the notes. I mean, even *The Godfather's* Michael Corleone waited awhile before whacking his brother Fredo. And "sibling repair" seems a likelier motive than insanity.

Here's an example of Rule No. 4: Don't stir the pot with other people's families.

No matter how annoying we find them, it is much worse for the blood relatives! So, smooth; don't incite.

Of course, Wifey is technically correct. Returning the response cards is sufficient. But if our spouses want to go a little further where their families are concerned, and respond personally, I can't see the harm in it—especially if they're the ones writing the notes. They may not accomplish much, but you never know. And it's a small price to pay to make them happy.

Maybe our spouses will return the favor and keep quiet when it's their turn to be annoyed with our families.

### Family Secrets: Just Say No!

Nothing drives a wedge like a secret!

So when our relations spill the beans about other family members—then ask us to keep mum—what should we do?

When Mom says, *Your brother has bedbugs. But don't tell him I told you.*

Or when Brother whispers, *Sister's marriage is on the rocks. But you didn't hear it from me!*

This behavior is extremely common among families—and seventh-grade girls. So just say no! Keeping secrets like these alienates us

Let's take a look at one last question:

Q My brand-new sister-in-law left her e-mail account open, so I read her messages to see what she had to say about me. Well, it wasn't pretty. She used an expletive to describe me to one friend, and called me a "high-maintenance pain" to another. I'm not sure where her animosity comes from. I know I violated her privacy, but I'd still like to discuss her anger. I want a loving relationship, but my feelings are so hurt I don't know if I can pretend ignorance. What do you think?

—*Stacey, Seattle*

How would you handle it? Review the "Mary, Mary, Quite Contrary" Program before you decide.

from each other, and unfairly prevents us from lending a helping hand.

Don't be shy: Let the secret-tellers know you don't play that way.

Next time Mommy (or Daddy or Brother or Sis) whispers, "I've got a secret," tell them you're not thirteen anymore—and stink at keeping them. That way, they can decide whether to keep the dish to themselves or enlist your non-secret aid in helping fix whatever problem needs to be solved.

Practically everything in life is easier to deal with once it's out in the open!

We've all done foolish things we regret—not auditioning for *American Idol* when it came to town, letting our sister talk us into bangs, invading Iraq. Trouble is, you don't seem the least bit remorseful about your error, Sister-in-Law. And I bet the self-centeredness that allows you to overlook your Watergate break-in, in favor of feeling wounded by your new in-law's private e-mails, may be part of what she dislikes in you. (Just a guess.)

Don't fess up—or defend yourself against the charges in her e-mails. (And don't involve your poor brother either.) Those are your burdens to live with, Harriet the Spy. You're already in the hole with this new sister-in-law, and I don't see you turning this episode into a knee-slapper in the near term.

Take her to lunch instead. Say, "I know we haven't gotten off to the best start, but I'd like us to be friends. Have I done something to upset you?" Then listen.

Remember, 50 percent of marriages end in divorce. With any luck, your brother's will be one of them!

# PART 6

Getting Nickeled-and-Dimed

# 16

. . . . . . . . .

# Money Isn't Funny

*Why Do You Think We Call It "Cold, Hard Cash"?*

One of my childhood friends makes a very good living, while I, on the other hand, am a musician who sleeps in a sleeping bag on my floor. This friend held his bachelor party in Las Vegas. I couldn't afford to make the trip, but he said, "I'll cover you." "Everything?" I asked. "Everything," he promised. All told, I spent about $1,400. But before receiving my total, he sent me a check for $500 with a note that told me not to argue, to take the whole amount. Now what do I do?

—Kieran, Washington

So it's more like, What happens in Vegas, stays on your Master-Card—at 19 percent interest!

Your friend said he'd cover you. So let's take him at his word, and hope he was just being careless when he lowballed your total expenditure. He took the same trip, after all. He can't be all that surprised by its cost.

Send him a note thanking him for the weekend, and include a breakdown of your travel and hotel expenses. Omit gambling losses and hooker fees. I'll bet he reimburses you the entire amount. But even if he doesn't, it's not the worst lesson: Talk is cheap, I'm afraid. And even with friends, it rarely pays to put our money where their mouth is.

"Nothin' says lovin' like somethin' from the oven."

The Pillsbury Doughboy is just a cartoon—pudgy and white, wearing a chef's toque and giggling every time an index finger pokes his chubby tummy. But give him this much: He's a cartoon who knows the value of a symbol, of letting a simple dinner roll stand for something greater in the scheme of things.

For however many shoppers the Doughboy has persuaded to buy those suspicious canisters of croissants or cinnamon buns—

you know, the kind you whack against your counter, and yeasty dough starts oozing out—he's reached a hell of a lot more of them with his heartwarming message, recasting half-assed pastry projects as the perfect embodiment of domestic love.

That's right! Pillsbury sells its wares as drizzled-with-icing symbols of how much our mothers (or the other lazy bakers in our lives) care about us.

Or in the Doughboy's own terms: Lovin' = Somethin' from the oven.

There's a very similar argument to be made about the relationship between friends and money, whether the cash in question is theirs or ours. Matters of the wallet are a frequent bone of contention between pals: *She never pays her share!* Or: *He always chooses places he knows I can't afford!*

But it's not about the greenbacks, folks—or not *just* about greenbacks anyway. A few dollars between friends could never generate so much angst. No, generally speaking, the way we treat our friends' money (and they, ours) stands for something bigger: It's a powerful symbol for the esteem in which we hold them, and often points up painful inequalities in the relationship.

So when things with one of your pals spiral out of control over moola, consider what the cash symbolizes.

Often:

## Money = Respect

Take VERY good care of your friends' cash—even silly, nominal amounts—because how we treat it is a powerful symbol of our respect for them.

For instance:

A friend owes me money—not a lot, but $15 is still $15. He borrowed it four months ago. He used to promise to pay me back every time he saw me, but now he doesn't mention it anymore. This irks me beyond belief, and I can't figure out why. In fact, the mere mention of his name fills me with disgust. Should I leave him a note or let this go?

"Don't Sweat the Small Stuff" is fine for bumper stickers, but this poor guy will have a heart attack if he "lets this go" for much longer! It's probably not about the $15 either. We blow more than that in an afternoon at the multiplex. No, the missing cash is a constant reminder of the borrower's failure to appreciate the loan—and value the friendship. And it's driving his poor friend crazy.

Next time our guy sees Deadbeat Donny, he should just tamp down his disgust long enough to ask, "Do you have that $15 on you?" Keep it calm; no need to turn an IOU into the Gunfight at the O.K. Corral.

And if he's too agitated for a quiet word, a note works too—though preferably not in red spray paint on the guy's front door.

Remember: There's no such thing as a small loan between friends.

So, Borrowers, if you can't keep track of little things like who you borrowed that fifteen bucks from, then don't borrow it from your pals! Because thoughtlessness with other people's money—even with paltry amounts—can cast long shadows over our relationships.

And Lenders, take note too: If unpaid loans are going to drive you up the wall, then don't make them to friends who are likely to be careless about repayment.

Of course, money issues are not always as simple as tit-for-tat loan transactions. The way we treat disparities in our financial circumstances can also create turbulence in our friendships.

Sometimes:

## Money = Aggression

I recently moved back to New York after trying my hand in LA for a few years. As a result, I make less money than my peers who stayed, and I'm living in a tiny rental apartment in Brooklyn. (I'll admit the discrepancy between my salary and my friends' makes me a little jealous.) But one friend has a habit of constantly interrogating me about "how I manage to survive" on such a meager salary. She'll even say things like, "There's a great new condo building, but I'm sure it's out of your league." It really hurts my feelings. I don't ask about her expenses. How can I get her to mind her own business without sounding defensive?

We're all a little insecure about where we fit into the scheme of things, financially (and otherwise). And a smidge of competition between friends is perfectly normal. In Germany, it's called schadenfreude; in America, *Desperate Housewives*.

So we sometimes comfort ourselves at the expense of our pals: I may not have it all, but at least I have more than you. It's only human, but it's also base and must absolutely be done—silently— in our heads! Unfortunately, some insecure folks, like our letter writer's pal, can't help lording their superior circumstances over others. This is incredibly hostile, and unless administered in minuscule doses, can be lethal to friendships. Our pals can help us in any number of ways, but buoying us up by their relative poverty should not be one of them.

It's the same from the other side of the equation: A little jealousy over our friends' better circumstances is only human, but if we're obsessed with it, it becomes a recipe for disaster. And frankly, better for all concerned to abort the relationship rather than stewing in jealous feelings.

So, assuming our twosome has a sincere basis for continuing their friendship (aside from using each other to jockey for position), a little pointed humor can help diffuse occasionally tactless behavior. The next time the richer pal rubs the poorer one's nose in the fact that she's not exactly living at the Ritz, our Poor Little Match Girl could try the following: "I know! I'm so poor I may have to move in with you any minute!"

Trust me, Richie Rich will never mention her living arrangements again.

Of course, discrepancies in income (or wealth) don't always spell trouble between friends. Sometimes the difference can point up the very best attribute of friendship—when:

## Money = Kindness

My friend and I went on vacation together. We shared a rental car and drove up the California coast to Big Sur. I knew it was an expensive trip for her; she's a graduate student, while I'm a doctor. But she insisted on splitting the costs of the trip evenly. We also shared the driving, and unfortunately, she got a whopping speeding ticket during one of her turns behind the wheel, even though I drove just as fast during mine. Can I offer to pay the ticket, or would that be insulting? Do our respective financial positions matter?

Of course our financial situations matter! And since no one could be broker than the state of California—with its massive budget deficits in every year—Dr. Do-Right should simply double the fine that's mailed with the ticket, since she was speeding too. (Only kidding.)

Let's applaud the good doctor's sensitivity to the money issue at hand: a simple expense will cause disproportionate hardship. Offering to pay the whole speeding ticket, simply because she can better afford it, is generous, for sure, but I wouldn't do that, especially since her friend was adamant about going Even Steven on the other expenses of their driving tour. Her grad student pal may take it as a show of pity, or feel uncomfortable drawing such a bright line under their different financial positions.

But here's an idea: How about a continuation of their fifty-fifty travel policy? That may be just the ticket (har har!).

Try, "Why don't we split the ticket just like we split all the other expenses of our trip? After all, it might just as easily have been me that was stopped."

Not only do we show our pal some kindness in that version, we also honor her desire to be our equal partner. Win-win, right?

And a final word to the wise: When speaking with friends about differences in our respective financial positions, make sure to highlight that these differences are only temporary. For instance, "I know you're strapped right now, but that won't be forever." It's true. Your friend may be a ramen-eating grad student today, but a high-priced lawyer in a couple of years.

It always pays to be optimistic about our friends' prospects, even in the case of would-be novelists and sculptors and ballerinas, whose chances for monetary success are only slightly worse than those of winning a Lotto jackpot. Still, optimism conveys our respect for their talents and belief in them.

What more could we want in a friend?

### When It's Even More Precious Than Money:
### Dealing with Our Friends' Special Stuff

It's not just money.

We've got to be careful with our friends' things too: when we (foolishly) borrow their cars or favorite cardigans—and especially when we throw caution to the wind and borrow sentimental stuff.

*For a special date, a friend lent me some costume jewelry that she'd worn at her wedding. I knew it had tremendous sentimental value, but somehow I still lost it. My friend tried to be cool about it, but I could see she felt awful. How can I make it up to her, other than buying her infant daughter some baubles when she gets married?*

> *Twinkle, twinkle, little fake,*
> *Until I lose you, or you break.*
> *But if you're borrowed, and I misplace you,*
> *Don't let me wait decades to replace you!*

Desperate times call for desperate measures, especially where prized junk is concerned. In this case, waiting twenty years to buy a replacement gift for your pal's infant daughter seems a tad underwhelming.

Why not head down to the jewelry store—right now!—and pick up a cultured pearl or two for your pal's Baby Girl? If you and your friend add to the collection from time to time, her daughter will have a wonderful necklace to wear at her wedding. And it won't be paste either!

You get the point: When you lose (or break) something that belongs to your friend, especially if it holds particular meaning for her, act as if the loss is as big a deal to you as it is to her. Replace it right away, and make a fuss about how sorry you are. That way, your pal will have a harder time hating you—and forgiveness is right around the corner!

So there you have it: When it comes to friends and money, be careful to show your pals the respect they deserve, while being mindful of your different circumstances too.

No need to turn that sawbuck into a loaded gun!

Q For my wedding, a good friend offered to do my makeup. I offered to pay her, but she said it would be her contribution to the wedding. As a thank-you gift, my husband and I bought her a large silk tablecloth. We later discovered that she's criticized us to everyone, complaining that we never paid her and that she hated our gift. When we see her, what do we do?

—Georgia, London, UK

A Well, for starters, try to resist your impulse to wrestle that eyebrow pencil out of her hands and scrawl "Psycho!" on her forehead.

You and your husband acted blamelessly. And given the frequent unreliability of stories passed from mouth to mouth, perhaps your pal did too. Maybe she said, "They didn't pay me, but they gave me an expensive gift. I don't really care for it, but it was very thoughtful of them." She's not completely hideous in that version. And it's not hard to see how an expert pot-stirrer could spin one tale into the other.

Next time you see her, say, "We're sorry to hear you didn't like the tablecloth. And if you'd like to be paid for your work, as we offered, just let us know." Your remarks will either be met with stunned (and innocent) disbelief, or the kind of guilty backpedaling that would give those doped-up American cyclists a run for their money. In either case, the legend of the lip liner will die a quiet death.

# PART 7

Getting Lovey-Dovey

# Crushing Hard!

*Surviving Your Infatuations*

Over the past few months, my sickly dog has put me in the frequent company of our vet. The care is great, but I've grown wildly attracted to him. He's friendly and kind—and possibly attracted to me too. But I see huge risks in vocalizing my interest. I don't want to jeopardize my dog's care or create unbearable awkwardness if he isn't interested. I feel like I'm going to burst! Am I doomed to lovesickness, or is there a way to tell him without losing my dignity?

—*Sophie, Pennsylvania*

Lassie, get help!

Fortunately, we've all seen enough episodes of *Grey's Anatomy* (as well as *Scrubs, ER,* and *Marcus Welby, M.D.*) to assure you that you are not going to burst. You've got a crush. That's good! Your wild attraction in the face of not really knowing him, coupled with the mystery of his interest in you, makes your vet an ideal object for romantic fantasies.

This may feel like life or death, but happily, it isn't. So let's dial back the drama. How about getting to know Dr. Bark-Good a little better before declaring your bubbling-hot interest in him? Invite him to coffee. It's not the sexy beach scene in *From Here to Eternity,* but you'll find out whether you have anything in common, aside from your sickly pooch.

Remember: There's no shame in asking someone out, even if he says no. You may want to hide under your bed afterward, but unless you're Halle Berry, I'm afraid that unrequited attraction is simply part of the human condition. And no reason for changing vets—a dry cleaner maybe, but never a vet.

---

**crush** \'krəsh\ *noun* [**ME** *crusshen*] An intense and usually passing infatuation <to have a *crush* on someone>; *also* : to act like a **damn fool** under the weight of one's passing fancy

---

I hate it when people begin speeches or toasts—or chapters in books—with dictionary definitions: "Merriam-Webster defines 'love' as . . ." Shoot me now, Maid of Honor!

But in the case of crushes, the etymology of the term so perfectly encapsulates the feeling of having one that I simply couldn't resist. According to the linguistic historian Michael Quinion, the word "crush" was a colloquial expression, in the early part of the nineteenth century, for a large dance or reception. These affairs were often hot and crowded (and the prevailing "statement skirt" of the era—of the large, fairy-princess variety—probably didn't help).

It was, literally, *a crush of people*. The first recorded use of the term comes from a letter written in 1832: "I fell in with her at Lady Grey's great crush."

From there, it was only a short hop to infusing the term for the party with those across-a-crowded-room romantic feelings that were often engendered there. At the time, these gatherings were the most common way for young singles to mix and meet. So the crush was the perfect venue for developing crushes, because the two requirements of crush creation were readily satisfied: (1) hearts quickening at the sight of (2) people we know a little, but not too well.

And so modern crushes were born: in the promise of romantic entanglement, but before we've discovered our potential partners' inevitable downsides—their emotional unavailability, for instance, or toenail biting.

In other words, when it's all good still!

People who are already in relationships might misremember "crushing" as a happy experience—what with all that delicious newness. But often, folks in the throes of crushes fixate on the quivering torment that lives alongside their attraction. We hear a lot about hands trembling and fears of bursting. Because people with crushes tend to behave as if the stakes of their crush are much, much higher than they really are. All that's going on is some lightweight social interaction (and frequently, not even that: It's just spying on people from a distance).

But don't tell that to someone with a crush!

They'll only be annoyed or claim, sighing, that you don't understand, because for them, their crush is a perfect seedling—and alternately, a terrifying man-eating plant.

So without further ado:

### The "Help Me! I'm Crushing" Guide for People with Crushes

1. May I express the oceanic depth of my feelings?
2. What if my crush isn't mutual—will I die?
3. How do I get the dude with the crush to leave me alone?

Let's start at the overheated beginning:

A new girl started working in my department. The more I see her, the more I feel like I was born to be with her. She's a fantastic person and really beautiful. I'm not sure how she feels about me, but I don't think I can keep quiet much longer. Can I share my feelings with her, or should I ask for a transfer?

Or here:

I take the train to the country on the weekends, and I frequently see a handsome guy who looks so intelligent and kind. Usually he's reading the paper (the same one as me!). The next time I see him, may I tell him he's caught my eye?

Try a third:

There's a girl who works out at my gym in the mornings. We both run on the treadmill and usually exchange a smile and a nod. She's very pretty, and I love her energy. Can I ask her for her phone number?

Do you see what's happening? (It doesn't take an eagle eye.)

Each of our letter writers feels attracted to someone. And that's a good thing! But rather than celebrating it for what it is—a nice first step—they project trumped-up qualities onto their crushes: intelligence, kindness, good "energy."

But it's just the attraction talking!

The writers don't even know these folks yet. So should they share their powerful feelings with the objects of their crushes?

Whoa, Nelly! Why not get to know each other first?

### Do NOT Conduct Your Crush from a Distance!

As soon as you feel yourself crushing, find a way—however small—to create real-life contact with the object of your crush.

Don't stew in the attraction, or let it morph into baseless fantasies of Einstein-grade intelligence or Mother Teresa–like warmth. Hold off on the big feelings—and declarations!—and take a few baby steps instead.

And no matter how fearful you may be of rejection, do not avoid interaction! Remember: You can't hit a home run if you don't step up to the plate.

So, for the guy who's crushing at work, bring your lovely colleague a coffee one afternoon. Get to know her over lattes! See if you have something in common (other than your paychecks), before declaring eternal love or inviting her on a romantic weekend to the Poconos.

The same goes for that gal on the train: How about sitting next to your guy the next time you see him, and asking what he likes to do when he gets to the country? (What if he's a taxidermist and stuffs dead chickens all weekend—or he's married, or gay?)

Ditto for the fellow at the gym: Don't jump from smiling at her in the mirror to asking for a date. Introduce yourself to Treadmill Trina and exchange some pleasantries. Is she easy to talk with? Ask her to spot you before asking for her number.

Don't get me wrong: I know how easy it is to get carried away. We've all done it, which is a reason not to do it again. So, before you swing for the fences, think small. Your feelings for your crush may have grown very large (in your head), but remember: You don't really know each other yet! Baby steps, okay?

Next up: You've taken it slow—or as slow as you were able—and the object of your affection still shot you down.

What then?

### *I Know It Hurts, but Let It Go! It Was Only a Crush!*

I met a great guy while training for the New York Marathon. We run together nearly every day, and we've also met for coffee a few times. But when I asked him if he'd like to go on a date with me sometime, he said I wasn't really his type. I feel that if he knew me better, he might change his mind. So I want to express my interest again. Do you think I have a chance with him?

Magic 8 Ball says, "Outlook not good." (Not that I don't admire the letter writer's moxie! Most of us, after rejection, want nothing more than to crawl under a rock.)

Unfortunately for Marathon Madge—as well as the rest of us—romance is the ultimate two-way street. And if the other guy isn't feeling it, we're going nowhere fast.

I know it hurts. But we made our pitch, and that took some guts. Still, there's no sense in pushing our case or risking the underlying friendship. Just lift your head high and carry on.

We've all been rejected before, and we've all gotten over it too. Because that corny saying of your mother's is true: Men (and women) are like buses. If you miss one, there's always another on its way. You just need to wait awhile.

Okay, last wrinkle: When the object of the crush is you!

### Don't Beat Around the Bush!
### Just (Semi-) Level and Move Along

My best friend's sister OBVIOUSLY has a crush on me: making me snacks, bringing me little gifts. But unfortunately, the feeling isn't mutual—at all. I don't want to hurt her feelings. So can I just avoid the issue, and wait until she puts two and two together on her own?

Of course you can, but that's not very kind of you! Having lived through a crush (or three) ourselves, why not be the person we wish other people had been? It doesn't need to be awkward. In fact, the lighter we keep things, the better.

When that gal with the crush invites us to the movies (for the third time in two weeks), just say, "Sorry, I've got a girlfriend." (Even though we don't, and our current romantic prospects are as sunny as Jennifer Aniston's.) She may be hurt for a second, but she'll get the point and move along, rather than wasting any more of her time on us. Or when the guy who's crushing hard asks if we'd like to have dinner sometime, try, "I barely get to see my [imaginary] children as it is!" I'll bet he backs off without any hard feelings. Because we've taken him off the hook, (semi-) directly and with kindness—and that's nothing to sneeze at.

Thus armed with these guidelines, go forth and crush to your heart's content!

### Girly Crushes and Bromances: The Platonic Crush

You're a happily married woman, but still you want to be Best Friends Forever with your brand-new lady ob-gyn. Or you're a Warren Beatty in the making who wants to be bro's for life with the new point guard from your basketball league.

So what?

Friend crushes are the best! When's the last time you met someone new that you actually liked? Well, you just did! So run with it: a new pal to chat with when you're bored at the office, maybe a partner in crime for your off-hours.

Just be careful not to inundate your crushes with too many calls or texts. (One a day is a good place to stop.) And try to keep your enthusiasm in check as you gauge their interest in return. Note: If they start hiding from you in the Pilates room at the gym, you may want to give it a rest.

Be sensitive to their romantic entanglements too. But a dinner for four may be the start of something big!

Crush on!

This guy I know has a ridiculous crush on me. My interest? Zero! Still, he's invited me to his ski house for the weekend, and even said I could bring a friend. May I go and just play dumb about the crush, since he's never actually mentioned it to me? Or will I spend the weekend being wooed and regretting it?

—*Sarah, San Francisco*

There are words, my dear, for people who parlay the romantic feelings of others into free ski junkets—and they are not "double black diamond."

Trouble is, regardless of what he's said, you know how this guy feels about you. You needn't be madly in love with him to accept his invitation, but you should have more than "zero" interest. You wouldn't want someone to play you that way, would you?

So no chairlifts, I'm afraid, unless—and this takes guts—you call your crushing pal to accept the invitation, and seamlessly work into the conversation that you're (a) already romantically involved, (b) holding out for Mario Lopez, or (c) unable to canoodle at high altitudes.

Then see if he wiggles out of the weekend.

# Breakups (and How NOT To)

*Learning from Slaphappy Scarlett O'Hara*

Q After twenty-seven years of marriage, my husband just left me for a woman young enough to be his late-in-life daughter. Even worse, he is bringing her to our club and all our favorite restaurants, where he gropes and fondles her like an adolescent. It's disgusting and humiliating for our children and me. I've asked him to take his tramp elsewhere, but he refuses. What do you think I should do?

—*Barbara, Southampton, NY*

A You mean, before or after you take him to the cleaners?

Listen, sometimes people go off the rails. (And by "people," I generally mean paunchy middle-aged men.) How else to explain your husband's rotten behavior—or the libidinous exploits of half the U.S. Congress? And when they go off track, I say, Stand back!

Since your husband could take his girlfriend to any number of places, his behavior seems intended to humiliate you—or impress the other old codgers at your club and favorite watering holes, who probably fantasize about robbing the cradle themselves. The more you protest, the creepier his behavior will become.

I'd steer clear of the club and find new restaurants, but just until your divorce comes through. Because unless there are extenuating circumstances you haven't mentioned—an airtight pre-nup maybe, or an attempt to murder your estranged hubby in his sleep—I'm assuming that the club membership, as well as the house and most of the larger bank accounts, will soon be yours anyway.

Get ready to rumble!

We've spent the last two hundred pages avoiding blowups: figuring out how to avoid as many bumps as possible on the bumpy road of life, and quietly ministering to the inevitable bruises we cause (and suffer) along the way.

But what do we do when the central romantic relationship of our lives crumbles into a million tiny pieces: when our live-in girlfriend starts making out with the creep from Sales at the firm's summer outing, or when our husband runs off with the nanny—three days before summer vacation begins?

### Crash! Bam! Pow!

By now, we've all heard those urban legends of lily-livered lovers breaking up via text message and Post-it. (And for the record:

Don't! Just man (or lady) up; tell them to their faces, and move on with your life.) But the more prevalent problem (at least judging from the nine zillion letters I've received on the subject at Social Q's) comes from breakups that are all too in-person—piercingly loud and bloodcurdlingly vicious, often premature, and occasionally involving shattered glass.

Don't get me wrong: I understand the allure of the nuclear breakup as well as the next guy. Screeching at your philanderer as you kick him to the curb can be fun (and good tension relief, to boot). So can shredding that lying she-devil's collection of skinny jeans—and maybe even changing the locks on both of them before they get home—all the while rocking out to Gloria Gaynor's "I Will Survive" (or Alanis Morissette's "You Oughta Know" or Marianne Faithfull's "Why'd Ya Do It?" or Pink's "So, What?" or—well, you know the drill). Good times, right?

I hate to be a wet noodle, but let's press that Pause button for just a second before you pull the plug. I know, I know—that's going to ruin the spontaneity of your hissy-fit breakup, but trust me, I'm thinking of your long-term best interests.

Because ill-conceived, nuclear breakups often end up causing us more trouble than they're worth.

And to prove my point, let's consider the case of Scarlett O'Hara, from that 1939 staple *Gone with the Wind*. If ever there was a more self-sabotaging gal in the annals of melodramatic cinema, I have yet to see her. Count on Scarlett to screw up every relationship (and breakup) that comes her way, especially if offered the possibility of slapping someone briskly across the face, which was like catnip to her.

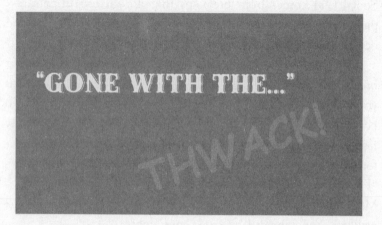

My aim is not to rob you of the pleasure of the bitch slap—not by a long shot. No, I simply want you to avoid impetuous breakups until you've taken the time to decide that that's really what you want.

In other words:

### Learn from Scarlett: Think First, Then Slap!

We all feel the occasional urge to decapitate our mates—or push them from high-story windows. It's only natural. (In fact, I'd be worried about the state of your union if you didn't.)

But just because the urge to maim is powerful, do not jump the gun and end your relationship! Don't let a rough patch convince you that the relationship is (or should be) over. Plenty of couples who find themselves on the rocks persevere, and are happy to live (and terrorize each other) another day.

Take Scarlett's love scene with Ashley Wilkes, early in the picture: They're sitting together in the pretty library at Twelve Oaks, and Scarlett is flirting her face off. Ashley, in turn, tells her that he has powerful feelings for her (good, right?), but also admits that he has feelings for too-good-to-be-true Melanie too (not so good—but not fatal either). What does our Scarlett do?

Well, fiddle-dee-dee, she slaps him across the face and hurls a vase across the room, shattering it—along with any prospect of a romantic relationship with Ashley. (No one wants to date a face-slapper.) And there's my point: The relationship wasn't even over, but Scarlett hastened its ending by letting it rip.

Do not make the same mistake: Never pull the plug too soon! It can be difficult (and sometimes impossible) to get it back into the outlet again.

Consider the following, from our present day:

My boyfriend and I have been living together for two and a half years. Last year, just when I thought he was about to ask me to marry him, he said, "This relationship isn't feeling right." I tried to discuss it with him, but he couldn't be specific—just cited his gut feeling. We continued living together, and things seem to be going better than ever. I even started to think he was going to ask me to marry him again—until last night, when I came home to the same thing: "Things aren't feeling right," and still he can't describe how. I've had it! My friends tell me I should give him an ultimatum: Marry me or pack up and get out. What do you think?

Get new friends! Who wants to strong-arm a marriage proposal?

Don't get me wrong, Long-Term Girlfriend: It might be extremely fun to pack up Ambivalent Amos's things and haul them out to the curb (especially after he's floated one of his vague "this isn't working for me" balloons). Hell, we might even set his stuff on fire! But after two and a half years together, why be so quick to pull the plug? We don't even know what the problem is yet!

Here's my hunch: The almost-fiancé is probably *this close* to proposing, but chickens out before taking the big step, and blames it on some vague "feeling" that the relationship isn't perfect. Well, whose is? (Either that, or he wants his gal pal to break up with him because he doesn't have the guts to do it himself.)

Either way, let's get to the bottom of it before cutting him loose. Try, "Honey, I'm committed to you and this relationship. But if you need help figuring out what the problem is—or whether you want to stay with me, let's try couples therapy." What have you got to lose? Never go for the nuclear meltdown when there's still a chance for a happy ending. Trust me, there's plenty of time for the flannel-shirt bonfire later.

• • •

Many times, romantic repair and reconciliation are neither possible nor of interest: The wife's a serial cheater, the beau is adamant about not having children when that's the only thing the girlfriend wants, or the mere sight of the onetime lover now makes us sick to our stomachs. What then?

### When It's Really and Truly Over,
### Wait One Second Longer!

But it's over, you cry—really! There's not a chance in the world that we're going to reconcile. Why can't I let it rip—now!—in a breakup so furious it will singe my soon-to-be-ex's eyebrows off?

Well, you can. But only after you're quite sure that you have everything you're ever going to need from this person again. (And the likelihood of that, I'm afraid, is pretty slim.)

Back to slaphappy Scarlett O'Hara for a quick example: Remember the famous childbirth scene with Prissy, Scarlett's vaguely hysterical housemaid? Well, in case you don't: Ashley's now-wife, Melanie, is pregnant and has gone into a perilous early labor, with no one to deliver the baby but—you guessed it!—Scarlett herself. The scene is fraught with danger: Will Melanie die? Will the baby? Our Scarlett is clearly no ob-gyn; she doesn't have the first idea what to do.

Just then, fortunately, Prissy brags that she's a real pro in the baby-deliverin' department, which is a huge relief to Scarlett until the actual birthing moment arrives, and Prissy delivers her most famous line: "I don't know nothin' 'bout birthin' babies, Miss Scarlett!"

Prissy lied. Turns out, she can't deliver babies like a champ; she's only got a rudimentary knowledge of obstetrics, which is still a great deal more than Scarlett has. So what does our self-sabotaging heroine do? Easy—in her trademark move, Scarlett hauls off and slaps Prissy across the face. *Thwack!*

That'll teach her, right? Well, possibly. But wouldn't it have been smarter for Scarlett to get the baby delivered *before* she slugged the only person in the room who has any idea how to deliver one?

Well, it's the same thing for modern-day folks in broken-down relationships: Don't pull the plug until you've identified another source of electricity!

Consider the following:

My wife and I live in a beautiful cottage (with a huge mortgage) by the sea. Unfortunately, the marriage faltered. My wife wanted to work on it, but I thought it would be smarter for us to call it a day. So we did, and my wife left. Problem is, I can't afford the mortgage payments without her contribution. Don't you think she should help with the payments until I can work out another solution?

Good question, Hubby, but you're a little late asking it. You should have thought about the mortgage payments *before* you gave your wife the bum's rush from your once-happy home.

And it's not just the mortgage. The same goes for the rest of us and (a) our prized collection of vinyl records that our estranged spouse will use as trivets; (b) our beloved twelve-year-old Labradoodle, which our ex-girlfriend wants to keep only to annoy us; and (c) even the financial settlement and custodial arrangements for the kids. You need to consider all these things before you walk out the door—or slam it.

It may sound mercenary, but when you end it, it's over! So hold off for a few seconds, and think through the logistics of your post-breakup world before you actually do your breaking up. (As for those shared mortgage payments that Hubby-by-the-Sea is looking for, I can only imagine where his dumped wife will offer to shove them!)

Many times, the endings of our relationships aren't as much endings as new beginnings. So unless you're sure that your breakup will be the last time you'll ever lay eyes on your former partner, and that you don't want or need anything from him (or her), ever again, just take a Xanax and suppress your urge to say, "You are the worst human being I have ever had the misfortune of knowing."

You can always say it later!

Remember: I'm not suggesting that you stay forever, not if your partner makes you miserable—just long enough to work out a sensible escape plan. (And for the record: Yes, I know this will be difficult, but no one ever said relationships were easy. And compared with breakups, relationships are a piece of cake.)

• • •

Okay, one more little detail for you to consider:

### The "Take Me Back, Rhett" Two-Step
### and Other Lousy Dances

When our relationships are falling apart, it's hard to believe that there's a chance (much less a desire) for reconciling with the very people who are causing us so much heartache and pain. How could we?

But strangely, the world is filled with men and women who want nothing more than to head straight back to the fount of their misery and reconcile with the very people they couldn't stand to be with just a few short months (or weeks or days) before. Maybe it's the devil-we-know syndrome, or maybe we selectively remember our former mates' good qualities, as we forget all about how they made our blood boil. Or maybe they're just looking better to us now that we've reacquainted ourselves with the filthy waters of the dating pool. Who knows? But it happens all the time. We might even know a couple for whom this second-chance reconciliation worked. Good for them!

For the vast majority of us, however, the "take me back" two-step only causes even more aggravation and hurt. Think about it: What's changed since the last time you weren't right for each other?

Let me drag you back to Scarlett and the plantation South one last time: In the final reel of the film, after Melanie dies—leaving Scarlett her big opening to bag Ashley Wilkes at last—Scarlett realizes that she never loved Ashley at all (huh?) and rushes straight to Rhett Butler to profess her eternal love for him and to beg for reconciliation.

No, thanks, Rhett says.

But I love you, Scarlett pleads.

"That's your misfortune," Rhett tells her as he walks out the door.

Good line—and good impulse, Rhett!

After suffering nearly four hours of film torture at the hands of Scarlett, Rhett knows that he will be better off starting over with someone new. And so will the rest of us!

Consider:

My boyfriend broke up with me a few months ago, but wanted us to remain friends. After weeks of avoiding him—because I was so hurt—I felt ready to see him again. But now, whenever he sees me in an upbeat mood, or whenever I talk about dating again, a sad look comes over his face, and he says he may never find a girlfriend as good as me. Sometimes he even asks if I'd consider getting back together with him. I'd like to maintain an honest friendship with him, but I don't know how to deal with his remorse or offers of reconciliation, especially after all my heartache. Would it be rude to tell him to shove off?

Rude? Probably. The thing to do anyway? Without a doubt.

This Yo-Yo Syndrome is as old as selfishness itself. As soon as our exes free themselves from the ties that bind—and we've begun to move on—they're not so sure anymore. Maybe we should get back together again? Maybe not?

I have no doubt that Breakup Boy is being honest—and so, probably, are the rest of our ambivalent heartbreakers. But that doesn't excuse the behavior. They know how badly we were hurt. What's more, it's a safe bet that this indecision merry-go-round

### When Friends Break Up
### Support 'Em but Steer Clear of Judgin'

We've all been there: sitting with freshly dumped pals, listening to them moan about their no-good exes as their teary eyes beseech us to join in.

Don't do it!

No matter how thoroughly finished with each other these two may seem—and no matter how objectively correct you would be in your criticisms—do not speak a bad word about the now-loathsome ex. Because there's still a chance that these two will reconcile, and where will you be then? On everybody's shit list, that's where.

Just sympathize with your friend's pain until the cows come home: "I'm so sorry you're hurting. I promise it's going to get better, but in the meantime, cry on my shoulder all you want."

Support her every way you know how, but draw the line at

will keep spinning until (1) they land new mates; (2) we reconcile, and they break up with us again; or (3) we pull the plug. I vote for (3)—at least in the near term. And unless you have a high tolerance for nonsense, you should do the same.

Listen up, breakup kings and queens: Once you've pulled the plug on your relationship—for better or worse—live with the consequences, unless you're absolutely sure that you want to be reconciled.

Not positive? Then keep moving.

trash-talking the ex, even if your pal pushes you to chime in (especially then!): "Wasn't it horrible the way he two-timed me?" Will you render judgment in that case? Absolutely not! Simply revert back to the agreed script: "God, I'm so sorry he hurt you that way," etc.

Got it? Good.

And what if you happen to be pals with both sides of the busted-up couple? Well, that's even more reason to stick to our script, as well as minimize the amount of time spent talking about the ex in question. Simply focus on your pals' pain, even when they try to elicit ridiculous promises from you: "You're never going to speak to her again, right?" Or: "Will you defriend him on Facebook?"

What do you say in response?

I knew you knew: "I'm so sorry you're hurting. I promise it's going to get better, but in the meantime, cry on my shoulder all you want."

And it will get better, I promise—even for friends of the loveless!

### And There You Have It, Breakups in a Nutshell

1. Never call it quits too soon.
2. Even when you're sure it's over, think through the aftermath before you pull the plug.
3. But once you have broken up, live with it.

No matter how hideous that looming breakup promises to be, or how impossible it seems that you'll ever get over it, just remember the immortal words of Scarlett O'Hara: "Tomorrow is another day!"

You will live to love again, I promise.

After living together in Europe for the last four years, I broke up with my girlfriend over Christmas, and I'm moving back to the States around Valentine's Day. I think it would be unkind of me to leave the day before, the day of, or the day after Valentine's Day. What's the best day to leave without making things even more dramatic than they already are?

*—Dion, Paris*

So is this what they mean when I see ads for "Romantic Getaways"?

Hate to break it to you, Casanova, but time heals all wounds *eventually*. Right now, after four years together and a Christmas kiss-off, your former gal pal is probably more interested in time (or an 18-wheeler) wounding all heels.

It doesn't matter when you leave. Personally, I'd rather go stag on Valentine's Day than have a pity dinner with an ex who dumped me. If you think your girlfriend takes a different view, ask her. Meanwhile, I consulted the wisdom of the ages (by listening to Paul Simon's "50 Ways to Leave Your Lover" three times in a row). The key, according to Mr. Simon, is "just get yourself free."

I suggest you do so with alacrity.

# PART 8

# Getting Through
# Our Big Days

# 19

. . . . . . . . .

# In the Spotlight (at Last!)

*Weddings, Bar Mitzvahs, and Our Other Big Moments*

Q My daughter is marrying a wonderful young man whose parents we've met only once. We enjoyed their company and seemed compatible with them. But the mother of my soon-to-be son-in-law has horrible teeth. The ones in front are twisted and black, and some are missing. There must be a psychological issue that keeps her from seeking dental help. But I'm concerned about the wedding pictures. It's my daughter's big day! I want everything to be perfect, and everyone to look their best. How do I communicate my concern without seeming like a monster?

—*Anonymous*

A Too late, Mom-zilla!

I'm sure you're no monster, but you do put me in mind of *Valley of the Dolls* author Jackie Susann, who famously barred people with disabilities (and plaster casts) from her book parties because "they just bring people down."

Here's the thing: Most of us have something, or occasionally two things, that keeps us off the cover of *Vogue*—possibly even you. So, better not to obsess about other people's crooked teeth (or saggy eyelids) lest they turn the tables and begin cataloging our little flaws.

Focus on the wonderful qualities that make Madam Chompers so compatible with you, instead of speculating on her psychological defects. Remember: You have the rest of your life to navigate with her, and a wedding album is no excuse for hurting her feelings. (And between us, none of the best wedding pics ever include the mother of the groom, right?)

Say, "Teeeeth!"

Who *doesn't* want to be a movie star? They're invited everywhere and rolling in dough. Or maybe a pop sensation with groupies and Grammys and grandstand arena tours? Or possibly a record-setting pro athlete who moonlights as a prizewinning novelist?

We're only human! Why wouldn't we wish for those things?

Still, the closest most of us get to nabbing the cover of *Us Weekly* is on that handful of occasions when we occupy the (much smaller) center stages in our workaday lives: at bar mitzvahs and confirmations, on graduation day, and most especially, at our weddings—marching down the aisle with every eye in the place trained on us. It's not so hard to understand our pent-up demand for attention on those Big Days, and our desire for everything to be perfect when we finally find the spotlight. There's a lot of glitter inside us, and not many chances to let it loose.

And there's the rub: Even though we don't get many of them, we still have to *try* to keep our Big Days in perspective, lest everyone we know smirks at us and rolls their eyes behind our backs.

Because:

## Other people care about our Special Occasions (just not as much as we do)

So, sixteen bridesmaids in $3,000 gowns? Nope—and nope.

A three-day bar mitzvah with round-the-clock film clips of the boy-of-the-hour? Sorry.

"But why not?" you cry.

I'll tell you: Because unlike the Academy Awards (and other red-carpet situations), there are no giant film and TV corporations dying to underwrite our Big Day—or billions of fans at home who can't wait to tune in. Giorgio Armani is not begging to clothe us. It's just our families and friends, and we've got to be careful not to overburden them.

Consider:

I'm getting married in a few months. The wedding is going to be awesome, but there are so many details to manage. So I called a friend from college, who's coming to the wedding, and asked if she would be my "wedding coordinator" on the day of the event, dealing with vendors and making sure things run on time. I thought she'd be excited, but she hemmed and hawed, then said her boss was looking for her. Now I feel offended. Can I disinvite her from the wedding?

Absolutely not! Coordinating a wedding is a job for family or besties—or better still, paid professionals. And unless Bridey has left out a piece of the puzzle (like her pal is the best-organized person in North America and loves nothing better than strutting her stuff), her request is too much to make of a mere college friend.

Call back and apologize: "Gosh, I get so carried away about the wedding. Can you forgive me—and promise to leave your *Wedding Planner* headset at home?"

# Remember: It's your Big Day,
## not everybody else's!

Inevitably, of course, Big Day celebrants will lose track of this fact. (It's our Big Day, after all!) And we can be consistently re-lied upon to monopolize the conversation, for months on end, with stories of our upcoming weddings, graduations, christenings, Sweet Sixteen parties, fortieth-birthday bashes, candlelit divorce vigils, etc. So when friends and families push back—occasionally criticizing us for acting selfishly about our special occasions—do not explode!

Just ask yourself:

# How would I feel if someone else were acting
## this way about their Big Day?

Don't worry if you're not the contemplative sort. Because it's a fair bet that our Moment in the Sun has probably gotten the bet-ter of us. Just backpedal like crazy and move along!

Unfortunately, this is not a perfect solution.

Many folks, in contemplation of their Big Day, will be unable to hold themselves back from thoroughly unreasonable behavior, even after we point it out as politely as possible. And expecting anything else from them is simply overoptimistic.

So:

## What to do when others drive us crazy with their Big Day-itis?

Try to be generous, that's what. And remember how hard it was for us to keep our own Big Days in perspective.

Consider these:

My friend strong-armed me into being a bridesmaid at her upcoming wedding, made me buy a hideous (and expensive) gown, then called it off! So far, she hasn't said a word about reimbursing me for the ugly dress. Can I scream at her now?

Or:

My sister invited me (with a guest) to her son's graduation dinner at a fancy restaurant, which she's turning into a three-ring circus. Then she retracted my plus-one when the party got too big. May I refuse to go?

Or:

My next-door neighbor invited my wife and me to his daughter's wedding, which sadly, turned out to be the same day as my father-in-law's funeral. Still, he gives us the stink-eye every time he sees us, as if we should have blown off the funeral for his daughter. Can I tell him off?

If you listen closely, you might just hear a rendition of "Here Comes the Bride" sung by Frankenstein's monster. Occasionally, perfectly reasonable people lose their grip on reality, and become selfishly absorbed in their own Big Events, while narcissistically ignoring us and our needs—sort of like Liza Minnelli at Radio City Music Hall.

Try to cut them some slack.

They're losing sleep (literally!) over seating charts and flower budgets. Or, in the (almost) words of Shakespeare's Hamlet: To have a chocolate fountain, or not to have a chocolate fountain, that is the question.

They'll be back to normal in no time.

And if they're not, we can take it up with them then—or hire an assassin.

### All This—and a Gift Too?

The Big Day folks get carried away. No question about it.

If they're not stealing one of our precious holiday weekends, they're planning a destination celebration, which means digging into our savings account for airfare, and hotel and restaurant expenses. (And in the worst of all possible worlds, they make it both a destination *and* our Fourth of July!)

But wait, there's more: These people expect a gift too!

Please don't give yourself an aneurysm. Remember: When friends invite us to their Big Day, they haven't created an obligation. It's always our *choice* to go. And when they choose expensive, out-of-town locales, they know (or should anyway) that not everyone will be able to afford it.

So if we really don't want to attend (or can't afford to), just let them know, as far in advance as possible: "I'm sorry we won't be able to make it. We (a) have a family reunion that weekend, (b) just can't afford it right now, or (c) are getting his-and-hers cheek implants that day." (You choose!) Just don't stall because you're chicken. Get it over with!

And when it comes to gifts, whether for destination celebrations or otherwise, we need only give what our hearts and wallets can comfortably spare. It's a token of the occasion, not an entry fee.

As a final note to all you folks who receive gifts in honor of your Big Day: Get those thank-you notes out as quickly as possible! The rest of us have put our own self-interest aside to give you the glitter and the spotlight that you crave. Nobody cares how busy you are afterward—just get the damned notes out!

Q At my son's bar mitzvah, over a year ago, a guest told me she had forgotten her gift at home and would give it to me later. I told her not to worry about it. A week later, we saw her at a birthday party. I asked the host if she had brought a gift. She had. For months afterward, every time I saw her, it was, "I still have your son's gift." Recently she invited us to her daughter's bat mitzvah. I struggled, but politely declined. And I did not send a gift, which is unusual for me. And still she says, "I still have your son's gift." What do you make of this?

—*Rhonda, Concord, MA*

Listen, Rhonda Wrapping Paper, I'm sure your pal's nonstop references to the never-given gift are really annoying. She probably never bought one, and the Edgar Allan Poe in her keeps forcing her to draw attention to the tell-tale guilt.

But take a step back. You invited her to celebrate a milestone in your son's life. And she was there with bells on. That's the important thing, right? Instead, you let this gift nonsense turn you into Miss Marple at a birthday party—sleuthing out presents—and made you decline an invitation to another event. That's the tail wagging the dog.

I'd much rather you screech into her driveway and demand she hand over her gift than let a measly $50 poison a relationship. Next time she refers to the present (and we all know she will), tell her, "I've heard about this gift more often than I've watched Sarah Palin shoot a gun. (And that's a lot!) Why don't we just let it go?"

But if she hands over a gift, make sure your son writes a thank-you note—pronto.

# 20

........

# Surviving the Holidays

*The Gifts, the Grannies, and All That Booze!*

Q My husband's grandmother loves taking pictures during holiday get-togethers. And nothing makes her happier than snapping an unflattering photograph. She's like a Hollywood paparazzo: giggling when she gets a shot of my double chin or my sister-in-law with a mouthful of pumpkin pie. Afterward, she sends albums of her offending photographs to the whole family. But this isn't how I want to remember our holidays. How can I tell her to cool it with the camera?

—*Christy, Ohio*

A (Gr)Annie Leibovitz sounds like a hoot-and-a-half, but I'm afraid that asking her to take more attractive pictures of you will only let her know she's hit her target—and possibly spur her to circulate her ugly photos to the national media.

But turnabout is fair play. So how about snapping a few candids of Granny—maybe slack-jawed and snoozing in front of a roaring yuletide fire? Or let slip that you've been researching old-age homes with excellent darkroom facilities—in Kazakhstan. She'll take the point.

But I'd the let the old bird have her fun. Just commission another of your rank to take kinder pictures. The beauty shots can serve as the official record of the holidays, and Granny's photo album, the blooper reel.

Whoever dubbed them "The *Twelve* Days of Christmas"—or the even brisker "*Eight* Nights of Hanukkah"—was wildly optimistic.

By my count, the holidays, as they're generically known, stretch all the way from the third week of November to the first week of January—from Thanksgiving until New Year's Day.

That's nearly seven weeks, or fifty days, of:

- Semi-relentless holiday partying, making us tired and hungover, yet still feeling vaguely excluded from the fantasy glamour-amas we wish we were invited to. You know, the ones with Oprah and Gayle, or Regis and Kelly—even Kathie Lee and Hoda.
- Spending way too much time (and even more money) on nonstop shopping at crowded stores and ugly malls for people we're fairly ambivalent about, while nursing a vague certainly that we're not getting a solitary thing we want in return (or finding the "It" toy that the kids in our lives are pining for).

- Seeing our families far too often and for much too long, but never once feeling as warm and cozy as they do on Walton's Mountain— "Night, John-Boy!"
- And though we haven't been hungry since polishing off that pound bag of Peanut M&M's on Halloween, eating and drinking with such wild abandon that our skinny jeans will be out of the question until sometime in April (at the earliest).

Sounds like fun, no?

Well, it can be. (Really!)

### Training for the Holidays

Here's the thing: The holidays are not a sprint. They're no fifty-yard dash that we can toss off with our eyes closed—or twenty minutes on the treadmill with our iPod and smartphone to keep us company.

No, the holidays are a long, hard season—more like a marathon.

And just as you wouldn't turn up at the starting line of a 26.2-mile road race without having trained for it, so too, is it pure folly to trip over Thanksgiving and just assume you'll make it to New Year's Day in one piece.

We must train for the holidays and create a plan for navigating them.

Lucky for you, I've got one:

**Your "Ho! Ho! Ho!" Plan for
Surviving the Holidays!**

**Ho(ld) back a little!** (If you try to do it all, you're going to run
out of gas.)

**Ho(ld) your tongue!** (The other guy is just trying to get through
the holidays too.)

**Ho(ld) the booze!** (You don't have to drink it just because it's there.)

Let's take a look:

Between us, my husband and I have eight siblings, most of them
with spouses or significant others. We buy trunkfuls of presents
every year, and I'm getting sick of it! Would it be incredibly rude
to suggest a Secret Santa arrangement, where each person buys
one gift, for a recipient chosen at random, with the emphasis on
humor and fun, instead of lavish spending? None of us needs a
thing.

After siblings hit the legal drinking age, I can't imagine not
moving to Secret Santa–land (or at least to token gifts). Who has
the time or money for full-on frosting?

No doubt, some families are thrilled at the prospect of buying
three hundred presents just because it's December, but I suspect
they exist mostly on the Hallmark Channel. Better to repur-
pose the money for the kids in your clan—or better still, your rent.

Feel free to suggest a Secret Santa plan. For maximum effectiveness, I suggest floating the idea at that supremely anticlimactic moment when the living room is strewn with wrapping paper and thoughts of Visa bills are dancing in every last head.

So here's our first "Ho!":

### Ho(ld) Back a Little:
### You're Less Likely to Run Out of Gas That Way!

When you see an opportunity for slowing down during the holidays, grab it! If your shopping list is too long (or you're invited to too many parties, or you're actually contemplating *two* cross-country trips in the span of six weeks to accommodate family and friends), don't!

Cut back instead. Sit down quietly and evaluate your holiday-party and travel schedule, as well as your gifting program. Be honest with yourself: Is it really reasonable to push yourself as hard as you have been? And once you've decided, don't be guilted into backing down. Remember: This is supposed to be fun!

I promise: A $100 gift, in your friends' names—to the American Cancer Society or the Worldwide Orphans Foundation—creates far more good in the world than that Shetland sweater or those shearling slippers you were going to buy. (Plus, you can make the gift online in just a few minutes, leaving plenty of time for a relaxing shiatsu massage!)

So take it easy on yourself, okay?

Now take a look at this one:

> Last Christmas, my sister gave me a beautiful pair of silver can-
> dlesticks. I love them. The only trouble is, I gave them to her two
> years before! At first, I thought she was joking, but when I real-
> ized she wasn't, I blurted out that she was really rude to regift a
> present that I'd put so much thought into, and that she'd hurt my
> feelings. Things have been a little frosty between us ever since.
> What should I do?

You mean, other than clubbing her to death with the candela-
bra? (Only kidding!)

I hope you'll forgive me for asking a little more of the victim,
but that's exactly what I'm going to do. No question, the regift-
ing sister was thoughtless and lazy—not to mention, tremendously
unlucky in giving those candlesticks straight back to their original
purchaser. (Can you imagine the odds?)

And I have no doubt that the letter writer's feelings were hurt.
But if the inter-sister frostiness is bothering her, our victim is going
to have to be the bigger person here, because the regifter doesn't
seem to have it in her. Do we really want to nurse frosty feelings
over a silly holiday gift? (I thought not.)

Try, "Let's put this candlestick nonsense behind us, Sis. I'm
over it. And I know how much pressure all that holiday shopping
can be. Maybe we should give each other the gift of not buying
each other gifts from now on."

Don't underestimate the pleasure of being "the bigger person" either. It often comes with a warm smugness (which must be hidden, at all costs, from the objects of our largesse).

Candlesticks? Solved.

But there's a bigger point here—our second "Ho!":

 ### Ho(ld) Your Tongue, If At All Possible: The Other Guy Is Just Trying to Make It Through the Holidays Too!

We all know how tough it is—decorating the house and buying the presents, making it to the kids' Christmas pageants (not to mention the airport) on time. We've been there, right?

So if friends or family members screw up, why not cut them some slack? If the present is obviously regifted, let it slide. If the Juicy sweatpants they give us are size XL (and we're a medium on our chubbiest day, thank you very much), keep quiet about it. If they don't make it to our Christmas party, but we have it on good authority that they went to that no-goodnik's buffet on the very same night, just let it go.

We're all just trying to make it through the holidays. Let's show some solidarity with our beleaguered loved ones and turn the other cheek. Plus, it'll probably be a funny story in March, when everyone's back to normal again.

Okay, moving on:

My office Christmas party is a big, boozy affair. Unfortunately, I drank more than my fair share this year, and vaguely remember approaching a really pretty girl in my department and stroking her hair. Now what should I do?

Step away from the bar, people!

Head directly to your colleague's office—first thing in the morning, before the coffee and bagel even—and apologize profusely: "I was so drunk. Can you possibly forgive me?" (Then pray the Absolut bottle didn't lead you into any other ridiculousness that you've "vaguely" forgotten!)

To all you boozers out there: It's still the office, even if there's a crepe-paper crèche hanging from the ceiling. And just because it's free doesn't mean you have to drink it!

"Ho!" No. 3:

### Ho(ld) Off on the Booze—Really!

With all the holiday parties come cases of booze—and the impaired judgment that go along with them. Glug! So think about imposing a two-drink maximum on your consumption.

You'll thank me in the New Year—when you're *not* searching for a new job because you goosed the head of Human Resources at your holiday party.

Remember: We've got a heavy calendar. Not only do we have to make it through *this* party, we also have to make it through the next one and the one after that. So take it easy on the hooch—and yes, that includes wine and beer.

And to all you flaxen-haired folk whose tresses might be stroked during the holidays—or bosses who might get an (unpleasant) earful from tipsy employees—please see "Ho!" No. 2: Try to let it slide. Under no circumstances should you put up with sexual

---

### Dealing with Nosey Parkers at
### Your Family's Holiday Table!

*So when are you two getting married?*

Or how about this one: *Still no job?*

Or my favorite: *Will we be hearing the pitter-patter of tiny feet anytime soon?*

Unlike hit-and-run holiday encounters with our friends and colleagues, holiday dinners with the extended family provide a special challenge: How to answer our relatives' incredibly personal questions about things that are NONE of their *^&%$# business! Well, just as the best military strategists have a number of battle plans at the ready, so, too, will we require a number of tactics for fending off our nearest and dearest during the holidays.

Deflection is always good. "Still single?" your aunt Ruthie may ask, with an attenuated frown and accompanying head tilt. To which you'll (or any other) harassment, but try to remember that we're all trying to survive the long, hard season.

So there you have it: With any luck—and a few deep breaths—you might just make it past the Thanksgiving turkey (and the endless leftovers), past the tinsel and the Hanukkah gelt, past New Year's Eve even, landing yourself safely in the post-holiday New Year.

Ho! Ho! Ho!

---

simply reply, "Is that a push-up bra you're wearing?" Just change the subject. Works every time!

Provocation works too. "So, when are you going to make me an uncle?" your mother's brother Saul may ask. "Speaking of kids," you'll say, "isn't your daughter getting out of prison any day now?" He'll be so annoyed that he'll forget his question about your procreation!

And remember, our relatives just want us happy—in most cases anyway. So the truth is also an option: "You know, for the time being, I like my life just the way it is."

Q I work in the publishing industry and receive lots of swag (and a tiny salary). During the holidays, I try to spread the wealth, giving friends some of these pricey goods. One friend has a habit of questioning the gifts' origins. "Did you get this for free?" she sneers, unwrapping some Chanel compacts or Shu Uemura cleansing oil. Does it matter that I didn't pay for her gift? Do I have to tell?

—*Martha, Venice, CA*

A Cast not your holiday pearls before swine, my dear, for those piggies will trample them—and ask whether you paid retail.

My hunch is that your sneering friend may feel uncomfortable unwrapping several hundred dollars' worth of glamour-osity when she isn't in a position to reciprocate. (I may also be wrong, and she might just be a big old witch.)

Here's what you do: Share your gift-giving philosophy with your pals, just the way you told us. It's charming and generous and makes perfect sense. No one wants their friends to lay out more than they can afford.

And once Grinchy Girl knows the lay of the land, I suspect she'll be smearing ritzy oil on her smiling face faster than you can say, "$150 an ounce!"

# Afterword

. . . . . . . . . . . . . . . . . . . . . . . . .

# So, What Do We Do Now?

Well, you've made it to the end. No matter what other troubles befall you (or what your sister-in-law calls you behind your back) at least you're not a quitter.

And that's going to come in handy. Because our world is only getting smaller and faster and even more tangled up. Whether you're at home or the office, on public transportation or out in the street, at the movies or the gym, or (thanks to our profusion of electronic gadgetry) all of those places at once, life serves up problems faster than a speeding bullet and a powerful locomotive combined!

And this much is sure: Occasionally you are going to say the wrong thing, your neighbor is going to do the wrong thing, your husband is going to tweet the wrong thing—generally, within ninety seconds of the call you receive from your son's school, telling you that he's just thrown up. Bumps in the road are inevitable, no matter how valiantly we try to avoid them.

But we can do our best. To minimize problems, if not prevent them; to not make the same mistakes twice; and to smooth over disruptions after they've hurtled by—and stained the living-room carpet. Our persistence can make all the difference in the world. Sometimes it can even persuade the people in our lives to try harder themselves. And what more can we ask for than that?

I hope I've given you some helpful tools for handling our new-fangled world, or at least some food for thought. So use that excellent head on your shoulders. And trust your instincts too, but not necessarily your first ones—because the impulse to snap and fight can come faster (and fiercer) than the impulse toward peace and kindness. Go with Door No. 2 whenever possible.

Remember, you're not alone. We're all in the same choppy boat. And you can always count on me and Social Q's. Look for us every Sunday in the *New York Times*. And who knows, maybe if we petition the publisher, she'll let me write a sequel. (God knows, I've got the questions for it!)

So, good luck out there. Or as my dad used to say, in a good-bye routine we honed over many years of school drop-offs, "See you in the papers"—leaving the punch line for me: "Among the cartoons."

# Acknowledgments

The most commonly asked Social Q—by far—is how to get folks to thank us. For wedding gifts and birthday gifts and Christmas gifts and dinners, for letters of recommendation and rides to work, and even (once, anyway!) for help in covering up an extramarital affair. We like to be acknowledged. And people want me to tell them how to make that happen.

It's simple! Be more like the team of folks who helped me produce this book—because it's impossible not to be grateful to them, or shout it from the rooftops.

So, thank you, to:

Mary Suh, Laura Marmor, Stuart Emmrich, Trip Gabriel and Joe Siano at the *New York Times*; Andy McNicol and Jennifer Rudolph Walsh at William Morris Endeavor; my amazing crew at Simon & Schuster: Kerri Kolen, the most inventive and stylish of editors, and the rest of the crack team: including Brian Ulicky (on publicity), Amanda

Ferber (on marketing), and Sammy Perlmutter (on bass); Jonathan Evans, my scrupulous copy editor; Ruth Lee-Mui and Jason Heuer, who gave the book its terrific look and feel; Michael Selleck, whose sales and marketing departments have been so encouraging; and publisher Jon Karp and his associate, Richard Rhorer, who preside over an amazing crowd.

And most especially, to Michael Haverland, for reading every draft of every column and chapter, and for being nervy enough to make excellent suggestions—usually after I think I'm done.

Many, many thanks to you all!

PG

# Illustration credits